Charles Heber Clark

The Fortunate Island and Other Stories

Charles Heber Clark

The Fortunate Island and Other Stories

ISBN/EAN: 9783744718585

Printed in Europe, USA, Canada, Australia, Japan

Cover: Foto ©ninafisch / pixelio.de

More available books at **www.hansebooks.com**

AN OLD MAN'S BLESSING. Page 126.

THE

FORTUNATE ISLAND

AND OTHER STORIES

By MAX ADELER

AUTHOR OF "OUT OF THE HURLY BURLY" "ELBOW ROOM"
"RANDOM SHOTS" ETC.

BOSTON
LEE AND SHEPARD PUBLISHERS
NEW YORK CHARLES T. DILLINGHAM
1882

COPYRIGHT, 1881,
BY CHAS. HEBER CLARK.

All Rights Reserved.

PREFACE.

THE custom which has ordained that a book shall have a preface is useful enough to writers who have to say to their readers something which could not properly be said in the body of the text; but it imposes a burden upon those who have no such communication to make. The author of the present volume considers that he may fairly perform the task by remarking that if the tales herein contained are not so amusing as others he has written, they will perhaps be found to be quite as entertaining, and possibly, in some particulars, more instructive. If they shall be received by the public with the favor that was found by the preceding volumes, the author will have reason to congratulate himself that they have achieved success of a somewhat remarkable character.

MAX ADELER.

CONTENTS.

	PAGE
THE FORTUNATE ISLAND	9
THE CITY OF BURLESQUE	107
AN OLD FOGY	221
MAJOR DUNWOODY'S LEG	252
JINNIE	311

THE FORTUNATE ISLAND

THE FORTUNATE ISLAND.

CHAPTER I.

THE ISLAND.

WHEN the good ship "Morning Star," bound to Liverpool from New York, foundered at sea, the officers, the crew, and all of the passengers but two, escaped in the boats. Professor E. L. Baffin and his daughter, Matilda Baffin, preferred to intrust themselves to a patent india-rubber life-raft, which the Professor was carrying with him to Europe, with the hope that he should sell certain patent rights in the contrivance.

There was time enough, before the ship sank, to inflate the raft and to place upon it all of the trunks and bundles belonging to the Professor and Matilda. These were lashed firmly to the rubber cylinders, and thus Professor Baffin was encouraged to believe that he might save from destruction all of the scientific implements and apparatus which he had brought with him from the Wingohocking University to illustrate the course of lectures which he had engaged to give in England and Scotland.

Having made the luggage fast, the Professor handed Matilda down from the ship's side, and when he had tied her to one of the trunks and secured himself to another, he cut the raft adrift, and, with the occupants of the boats, sorrowfully watched the brave old "Morning Star" settle down deeper and deeper into the water; until at last, with a final plunge, she dipped beneath the surface and disappeared.

The prospect was a cheerless one for all of the party. The sea was not dangerously rough; but the captain estimated that the nearest land was at least eight hundred miles distant; and, although there were in the boats and upon the raft provisions and water enough for several days, the chance was small that a port could be made before the supplies should be exhausted. There was, moreover, almost a certainty that the boats would be swamped if they should encounter a severe storm.

The Professor, for his part, felt confident that the raft would outlive any storm; but his shipmates regarded his confidence in it as an indication of partial insanity.

The captain rested his expectations of getting

ashore chiefly upon the fact that they were in the line of greatest travel across the Atlantic, so that they might reasonably look to meet, within a day or two, with a vessel of some kind which would rescue them.

As the night came on, it was agreed that the boats and the raft should keep together, and the captain had provided a lantern, which was swung, lighted, aloft upon an oar, so that the position of his boat could be determined. The Professor, with his raft under sail, steered along in the wake of the boats for several hours, Matilda, meanwhile, sleeping calmly, after the exciting and exhausting labors of the day, upon a couple of trunks.

As the night wore on, a brisk wind sprang up, and shortly afterward the light upon the captain's boat for some reason disappeared. The Professor was somewhat perplexed when he missed it, but he concluded that the safest plan would be to steer about upon the course he had hitherto held, and then to communicate with the boats if they should be within sight in the morning.

The wind increased in force about midnight, and the raft rolled and pitched in such a manner that the Professor's faith in it really lost some of its force. Several times huge waves swept over it, drenching the Professor and his daughter, and filling them with grave apprehensions of the result if the storm should become more violent.

Even amid the peril, however, Professor Baffin could not but admire the heroic courage and composure of Matilda, who sat upon her trunk, wet and shivering with cold, without showing a sign of fear, but trying to encourage her father with words of hope and cheer.

When the dawn came, dim and gray, the gale abated its force, and although the sea continued rough, the raft rode the waves more buoyantly and easily. Producing some matches from his waterproof box, the Professor lighted the kerosene-lamp in the tiny stove which was in one of the boxes; and then Matilda, with water from the barrel, began to try to make some coffee. The attempt seemed to promise to be successful, and while the process was going on, the Professor looked about for the boats. They could not be seen. The Professor took out his glass and swept the horizon. In vain; the boats had disappeared completely; but the Professor saw something else that attracted his attention, and made his heart for a moment stop beating.

Right ahead, not distinctly outlined, but visible in a misty sort of way, he thought he discerned land!

At first he could not believe the evidence of his sight. The captain, an expert navigator, had assured him that they were eight hundred miles from any shore. But this certainly looked to the Professor very much like land. He examined it through his glass. Even then the view was not clear enough to remove all doubts, but it strengthened his conviction; and when Matilda looked she said she knew it was land. She could trace the outline of a range of hills.

"Tilly," said the Professor, "we are saved! It *is* the land, and the raft is drifting us directly towards it. We cannot be sufficiently thankful, my child, for this great mercy! Who would have expected it? Taken altogether, it is the most extraordinary circumstance within my recollection."

"Captain Duffer must have made a miscalculation," said Tilly. "The ship must have been off of her course when she sprang a leak."

"It is incomprehensible how so old a sailor could have made such a blunder," replied the Professor. "But there the land is; I can see it now distinctly. It looks to me like a very large island."

"Are you going ashore at once, pa?"

"Certainly, dear; that is, if we can make a landing through the breakers."

"Suppose there are cannibals on it, pa? It would be horrid to have them eat us!"

"They would have to fatten us first, darling; and that would give us an opportunity to study their habits. It would be extremely interesting!"

"But the study would be of no use if they should eat us!"

"All knowledge is useful, Tilly; I could write out the results of our observations, and probably set them adrift in a bottle!"

"It is such a dreadful death!"

"Try to look at it philosophically! There is really nothing more unpleasant about the idea of being digested than there is about the thought of being buried."

"O, pa!"

"No, my child! It is merely a sentiment. If I shall be eaten, and we have volition after death, I am determined to know how I agreed with the man who had me for dinner! Tilly, I have a notion that you would eat tender!"

"Pa, you are simply awful!"

"To me, indeed, there is something inspiring in the thought that my physical substance, when I have done with it, should nourish the vitality of another being. I don't like to think that I may be wasted."

"You seem as if you rather hoped we should find savage cannibals upon the island!"

"No, Tilly; I hope we shall not. I believe we shall not. Man-eaters are rarely found in this latitude. My impression is that the island is not inhabited at all. Probably it is of recent volcanic origin. If so, we may have a chance to examine a newly-formed crater. I have longed to do so for years."

"We might as well be eaten as to be blown up and burned up by a volcano," said Matilda.

"It would be a grand thing, though, to be permitted to observe, without interruption, the operation of one of the mightiest forces of nature! I could make a magnificent report to the Philosophical Society about it; that is, if we should ever get home again."

"For my part," said Matilda, "I hope it contains neither cannibals nor volcanoes; I hope it is simply a charming island without a man or a beast upon it."

"Something like Robinson Crusoe's, for example! I have often thought I should like to undergo his experiences. It must be, to an inquiring mind, exceedingly instructive to observe in what manner a civilized man, thrown absolutely upon his own resources, contrives to conduct his existence. I could probably enrich my lecture upon Sociology if we should be compelled to remain upon the island for a year or two."

"But we should starve to death in that time!"

"So we should; unless, indeed, the island produces fruits of some kind from its soil. I think it does. It seems to be covered with trees, Tilly, doesn't it?"

"Yes," said Matilda, looking through the glass. "It is a mass of verdure. It is perfectly beautiful. I believe I see something that looks like a building, too."

"Impossible! you see a peculiar rock formation, no doubt; I shan't be surprised if there is enough in the geological formation of the island to engage my attention so long as we remain."

"But what am I to do, meantime?"

"You? Oh, you can label my specimens and keep the journal; and maybe you might hunt around for fossils a little yourself."

The raft rapidly moved toward the shore, and the eyes of both of the voyagers were turned toward it inquiringly and eagerly. Who could tell how long the island might be their home, and what strange adventures might befall them there?

"The wind is blowing right on shore, Tilly," said the Professor. "I will steer straight ahead, and I shouldn't wonder if we could shoot the breakers safely. Isn't that a sand-beach right in front there?" inquired the Professor, elevating his nose a little, to get his spectacles in focus. "It looks like one."

"Yes, it is," replied Matilda, looking through her glass.

"First-rate! Couldn't have been better. There, we will drive right in. Tilly, hoist my umbrella, so as to give her more sail!"

The raft fairly danced across the waves under the increased pressure, and in a moment or two it was rolling in the swell just outside of the line of white breakers. Before the Professor had time to think what he should do to avoid the shock, a huge wave uplifted the raft and ran it high upon the beach with such violence as to compel the Professor to turn a somersault over a trunk. He recovered himself at once, and replacing his spectacles he proceeded, with the assistance of Matilda, to pull the raft up beyond the reach of the waves.

Then, wet and draggled, with sand on his coat, and his hat knocked completely out of shape, he stood rubbing his chin with his hand, and thoughtfully observing the breakers.

"Extraordinary force, Tilly, that of the ocean surf,— clear waste, too, apparently. If we stay here long enough, I must try to find out the secret of its motion."

"Hadn't we better put on some dry clothing first?" suggested Miss Baffin, "and examine the surf afterwards? For my part I have had enough of it."

"Certainly! Have you the keys of the trunks? Everything soaking wet, most likely."

When the trunks were unfastened, the Professor was delighted to find that the contents were perfectly dry. Selecting some clothing for himself, he went behind a huge rock and proceeded to dress. Matilda, after looking carefully about, retreated to a group of trees, and beneath their shelter made her toilette.

"Isn't this a magnificent place?" said the Professor, when Matilda, nicely dressed, came out to where he was standing by the raft.

"Perfectly lovely."

"Noble trees, rich grass, millions of wild flowers, birds twittering above us, a matchless sky, a bracing air, and — why, halloa! there's a stream of running water! We must have a drink of that, the very first thing. Delicious, isn't it?" asked the Professor, when Miss Baffin, after drinking, returned the cup to him.

"It is nectar."

"I tell you what, Tilly, I am not sure that it wouldn't be a good thing to be compelled to live here for two or three years. The vegetation shows that we are in a temperate latitude, and I know I can find or raise enough to eat in such a place as this."

"Why, pa, look there!"

"Where?"

"Over there. Don't you see that castle?"

"Castle? No! What! Why, yes, it is! Bless my soul, Tilly, the place is inhabited!"

"Who would have thought of finding a building like that on an island in mid-ocean?"

"It is the most extraordinary circumstance, taking it altogether, that ever came under my observation," said the Professor, looking towards the distant edifice. "So far as I can make out, it is a castle of an early period."

"Mediæval?"

"Well, not later than the seventh or eighth century, at the farthest. Tilly, I feel as if something remarkable was going to happen."

"Pa, you frighten me!"

"No, I mean something that will be extraordinarily interesting. I know it. The voice of instinct tells me so. Have you your journal with you?"

"It is in the trunk."

"Get it and your lead-pencils. We will drag the baggage further up from the water, and then we will push towards the castle. I am going to know the date of that structure before I sleep to-night."

"There can hardly be any danger, I suppose?" suggested Miss Baffin, rather timidly.

"Oh, no, of course not; I have my revolver with me. Let me see; where is it? Ah, here. And the cartridges are waterproof. I think I will put a few things in a valise, also. We might find the castle empty, and have to depend upon ourselves for supper."

The Professor then let the air out of the raft, and folded the flattened cylinders together.

When the valise was ready, the Professor grasped it, shouldered his umbrella, and said, "Now, come, darling, and we will find out what all this means."

The pair started along a broad path which ran by the side of the stream, following the course of the brook, and winding in and out among trees of huge girth and gigantic height. Birds of familiar species flitted from branch to branch before them, as if to lead them on their way; now and then a brown rabbit, after eyeing them for a moment with quivering nostrils, beat a quick tattoo upon the ground with his hind legs, then threw up his tail and whisked into the shrubbery. Gray squirrels scrambled around the trunks of the trees to look at them, and now and then a screaming, blue-crested kingfisher ceased his complaining while he plunged into one of the pools of the rivulet, and emerged with a trout in his talons.

It was an enchanting scene; and Miss Baffin enjoyed it thoroughly as she stepped blithely by the side of her father, who seemed to find especial pleasure in discovering that the herbage, the trees, the rocks, and all the other natural objects, were precisely like those with which he had been familiar at home.

After following the path for some time, the pair came to a place where the brook widened into a great pool, through which the water went sluggishly, bearing upon its surface bubbles and froth, which told how it had been tossed and broken by rapid descents over the rocks in some narrow channel above. Here the Professor stopped to observe an uncommonly large and green bullfrog, which sat upon a slimy stone a few yards away, looking solemnly at him.

During the pause, they were startled to hear a voice saying to them, —

"Good morrow, gentle friends."

Matilda uttered a partly-suppressed scream, and even the Professor jumped backward a foot or two, in astonishment.

Looking toward the place from which the voice came, they saw an old man with gray hair and beard lifting a large stone pitcher, which he had been filling from the pool. He was dressed in a long and rather loose robe, which reached from his shoulders to his feet, and which was gathered about his waist with a knotted cord. This was his entire costume, for his feet were bare, and he wore no hat to hide the rich masses of hair which fell to his shoulders. As he offered his salutation, he raised his pitcher until he stood upright, and then he looked at the Professor and Miss Baffin with a pleasant smile, in which there were traces of curiosity.

"Good afternoon," returned the Professor, after a moment's hesitation; "how are you?"

"Are you not strangers in this land?" asked the old man.

"Well, yes," said the Professor, briskly, with a manifest purpose to be sociable; "we have just come ashore down here on the beach. Shipwrecked, in fact. This is my daughter. Let me introduce you. My child, allow me to make you acquainted with — with — beg pardon, but I think you did not mention your name."

"I am known as Father Anselm."

"Ah, indeed! Matilda, this is Father Anselm. A clergyman, I suppose?"

"I am a hermit; my cell is close at hand. You will be welcome there if you will visit it."

"A hermit! Living in a cell! Well, this *is* surprising! We shall be only too happy to visit you, if you will permit us. Delightful, isn't it, dear? We will obtain some valuable information from the old gentleman."

The Hermit, with the pitcher poised upon his shoulder, led the way, and he was closely followed by the Professor and by Matilda, who regarded the proceeding rather with nervous apprehension. The Hermit's cell was a huge cave, excavated from the side of a hill. The floor was covered with sprigs of fragrant evergreens. A small table stood upon one side of the apartment; beside it was a rough bench, which was the only seat in the room. A crucifix, a candle, a skull, an hour-glass, and a few simple utensils were the only other articles to be seen.

The Hermit brought forward the bench for his visitors to sit upon, and then, procuring a cup, he offered each a drink of water.

The Professor, hugging one knee with interlocked fingers, seemed anxious to open a conversation.

"Pardon me, sir, but do I understand that you are a clergyman; that is to say, some sort of a teacher of religion?"

"I belong to a religious order. I am a recluse."

"Roman Catholic, I presume?" said the Professor, glancing at the crucifix.

"Your meaning is not wholly clear to me," replied the Hermit.

"What are your views? Do you lean to Calvinism, or do you think the Arminians, upon the whole, have the best of the argument?"

"The gentleman does not understand you, pa," said Miss Baffin.

"Never mind, then; we will not press it. But I should like very much if you would tell us something about this place; this country around here," said the Professor, waving his hand towards the door.

"Let me ask first of the misadventure which cast you unwillingly upon our shores?" said the Hermit.

"Well, you see, I sailed from New York on the twenty-third of last month, with my daughter here, to fulfil an engagement to deliver a course of lectures in England."

"In England!" exclaimed the Hermit, with an appearance of eager interest.

"Yes, in England. I am a professor, you know, in an American university. When we were about half way across, the ship sprang a leak, from some cause now unknown. My daughter and I got off with our baggage upon a life-raft, which I most fortunately had with me. The rest of the passengers and the crew escaped in the boats. I became separated from them, and drifted here. That is the whole story."

"I comprehend only a part of what you say," replied the Hermit. "But it is enough that you have suffered; I give you hearty welcome."

"Thank you. And now tell me where I am."

"You spoke of England a moment ago," said the Hermit. "Let me begin with it. Hundreds of years ago, in the time of King Arthur, of noble fame, it happened, by some means even yet not revealed to us, that a vast portion of that island separated from the rest, and drifted far out upon the ocean. It carried with it hundreds of people —noble, and gentle, and humble. This is that country."

"In-*deed!*" exclaimed the Professor. "This? This island that we are on? Amazing!"

"It is true," responded the Hermit.

"Why, Tilly, do you hear that? This is the lost Atlantis! We have been driven ashore on the far-famed Fortunate Island! Wonderful, isn't it? Taking every thing into consideration, I must say this certainly is the most extraordinary circumstance I ever encountered!"

"Nobody among us has ever heard anything from England or of it, excepting through tradition. No ship comes to our shores, and those of us who have builded boats and gone away in search of adventure have never come back. Sometimes I think the island has not ended its wanderings, but is still floating about; but we cannot tell."

"But, my dear sir," said the Professor, "you can take your latitude and longitude at any time, can't you?"

"Take what?"

"Your latitude and longitude! Find out exactly in what part of the world you are?"

"I never heard that such a thing was done. None of our people have that kind of learning."

"Well, but you have schools and colleges, and you acquire knowledge, don't you?"

"We have a few schools; but only the low-born children attend them, and they are taught only what their fathers learned. We do not try to know more. We reverence the past. It is a matter of pride among us to preserve the habits, the manners, the ideas, the social state which our forefathers had when they were sundered from their nation."

"You live here pretty much as King Arthur and his subjects lived?"

"Yes. We have our chivalry; our knight errants; our tournaments; our castles — everything just as it was in the old time."

"My dear," said the Professor to Miss Baffin, "the wildest imagination could have conceived nothing like this. We shall be afforded an opportunity to study the middle ages on the spot."

"Sometimes," said the Hermit, gravely, "I have secret doubts whether our way is the best, whether in England and the rest of the world men may not have learned while we have remained ignorant; but I cannot tell. And no one would be willing to change if we could know the truth."

"My friend," said the Professor, with a look of compassion, "the world has gone far, far ahead of King Arthur's time! It has almost forgotten that there ever was such a time. You would hardly believe me, at any rate you would not understand me, if I should tell you of the present state of things in the world. But if I stay here I will try to enlighten you gradually. I feel as I had been sent here as a missionary for that very purpose."

"Do you come from England?"

"Oh, no! I was going thither. I came from the United States. You never heard of them, of course. They are a land right across the ocean from England, about three thousand miles."

"Discovered by a man named Columbus," said Miss Baffin.

"Your dress is an odd one," continued the Hermit. "Are you a fighting man?"

"A fighting man! Oh, no, of course not. I'm a Professor."

"Then this is not a weapon that you carry."

"Bless my soul, my dear sir! Why, this is an umbrella! Tilly, we have to deal with a very primitive condition of things here. It is both entertaining and instructive."

"What is it for?"

"I will show you. Suppose it begins to rain, I untie this string and open the umbrella, *so!* Now don't be alarmed! It is perfectly harmless, I assure you!"

The holy man had retreated suddenly into the furthest recess of the cell.

"While it rains I hold it in this manner. When it clears, I shut it up, *thus*, and put it under my arm."

"Wonderful! wonderful!" exclaimed the Hermit. "I thought it was an implement of war. The world beyond us evidently has surpassed us."

"This is nothing to the things I will show you," said the Professor. "I see you have an hour-glass here. Is this the only way you have of recording time?"

"We have the sun."

"No clocks or watches?"

"I do not know what they are."

"Tilly, show him your watch. This is the machine with which we tell time."

"Alive, is it?" asked the Hermit.

The Professor explained the mechanism to him in detail.

"You are indeed a learned man," said the recluse. "But I have forgotten a part of my duty. Will you not take some food?"

"Well," said the Professor, "if you have anything about in the form of a lunch, I think I could dispose of it."

"I am awfully hungry," said Miss Baffin.

The Hermit produced a piece of meat, and hanging it upon a turnspit he gathered a few sticks and placed them beneath it. The Professor watched him closely; and when the holy man took in his hands a flint and steel with which to ignite the wood, the Professor exclaimed, —

"One moment! Let me start that fire for you?"

Taking from his pocket an old newspaper, he put it beneath the sticks; then from his match-box he took a match, and striking it there was a blaze in a moment.

The Hermit crossed himself and muttered a prayer at this performance.

"No cause for alarm, I assure you," said the Professor.

"You must be a wizard," said the Hermit.

"No; I did that with what we call a match; like this one. There is stuff on the end which catches fire when you rub it," and the Professor again ignited a match.

"I never could have dreamed that such a thing

could be," exclaimed the recluse. "You will be regarded by our people as the most marvellous magician that ever lived."

The Professor laughed.

"Oh," said he, "I will let them know it is not magic. We must clear all that nonsense away. Tilly, I feel that duty points me clearly to the task of delivering a course of lectures upon this island."

During the repast, the Hermit, looking timidly at Professor Baffin, said, —

"Would it seem discourteous if I should ask you another question?"

"Certainly not. I shall be glad to give you any information you may want."

"What, then," inquired the Hermit, "is the reason why you protect your eyes with glass windows?"

"These," said the Professor, removing his spectacles, "are intended to improve the sight. I cannot see well without them. With them I have perfect vision. Tilly, make a memorandum in the journal that my first lecture shall be upon Optics."

"Pa, I wish we could learn something about the castle we saw," observed Miss Baffin.

"Oh, yes; by the way, Father Anselm," said the Professor, "we observed an old-fashioned castle over yonder, as we came here. Can you tell me anything about it?"

"The castle," replied the Hermit, "is the home

and the stronghold of Sir Bors, Baron of Lonazep. He is a great and powerful noble, much feared in this country."

"Any family?" inquired the Professor.

"He has a gallant son, Sir Dinadan, as brave a knight as ever levelled lance, and a beautiful daughter, Ysolt. Both are unmarried; but the fair Ysolt fondly loves Sir Bleoberis, to whom, however, the Baron will not suffer her to be wedded, because Sir Bleoberis, though bold and skilful, has little wealth."

"Human nature, you observe, my child, is the same everywhere. We have heard of something like this at home," remarked the Professor to his daughter.

"Ysolt is loved also by another knight, Sir Dagonet. He has great riches, and is very powerful; but he is a bad and dangerous man, and the Baron will not consent to give him Ysolt to wife. These matters cause much strife and much unhappiness."

"It's the same way with us," observed the Professor; "I have known lots of such cases."

"I hope we shall stay here long enough to see how it all turns out," said Miss Baffin.

"Of course," replied the Professor. "You hated the island when you thought it might promote the interests of science. But some lovers' nonsense would keep you here willingly for life. Just like a woman."

"The King," said the Hermit, "has espoused the cause of Sir Bleoberis, and we hope he may win the lady for the knight whom she loves."

"The King, eh? Then you have a monarchical government?"

"We have eleven kings upon this island."

"All reigning?"

"Yes."

"How many people are there in the whole island?"

"No one knows, exactly. One hundred thousand, possibly."

"Not ten thousand men apiece for the kings! Humph! In my country we have a million men in one town, and nobody but a common man to rule them."

"Incredible!"

"And what is the name of your particular king,— the one who is lord of this part of the country?"

"King Brandegore; a wise, and good, and valiant monarch."

"Tilly," said the Professor, "you might as well jot that down. Eleven kings on the island, and King Brandegore running this part of the government. I must get acquainted with him."

When the meal was finished the Professor said to the recluse, —

"Do you allow smoking?"

"Smoking!"

"Pray excuse me! I forgot. If you will permit me, I will introduce you to another of the practices of modern civilization."

Then the Professor lighted a cigar, and, sitting on the bench in a comfortable position, with his back against the wall of the cave, he began to puff out whiffs of smoke.

The Hermit, with a look of alarm, was about to ask for an explanation of the performance, when loud cries were heard outside of the cave mingled with frightened exclamations from a woman.

The occupants of the cavern started to their feet, just as a beautiful girl, dressed in a quaint but charming costume, ran into the doorway in such haste that she dashed plump up against the Professor, who caught her in his arms.

For a moment she was startled at seeing two strangers in a place where she had thought to encounter none but the Hermit; but her dread of her pursuer overcame her diffidence, and, clinging to the Professor, she exclaimed, —

"Oh, save me! save me!"

"Certainly I will," said the Professor, soothingly, as his arm tightened its clasp about her waist. "What's the matter? Don't be afraid, my child. Who is pursuing you?"

The Professor was not displeased at the situation in which he found himself. The damsel was fair to see, and the head which rested, in what seemed to him sweet confidence, upon his shoulder, was crowned with golden hair of matchless beauty. Even amid the intense excitement of the moment the reflection flashed through the Professor's mind that he was a widower, and that Matilda had always expressed a willingness to try to love a stepmother.

"My father! The Baron! He threatens to kill me," sobbed the maiden, and then, tearing herself away from the Professor in a manner which struck him as being, to say the least, inconsiderate, she flew to Father Anselm and said, "You, holy father, will save me."

"I will try, my daughter; I will try, replied the Hermit. And then, turning to the Professor he said, "It is Ysolt."

"Ah!" said the Professor, "the Baron's daughter. May I ask you, miss, what the old gentleman is so excited about? It is not one of the customs here for indignant parents to chase their children around the country, is it?"

"I had gone from the castle," said the damsel, partly to the Hermit and partly to Professor Baffin, "to meet Sir Bleoberis at the trysting-place. My father was watching me, and as I neared the spot he rushed toward me with a drawn sword, threatening to kill me."

"It is an outrageous shame!" exclaimed the Professor, sympathetically.

"I eluded him," continued the sobbing girl, "and flew towards this place. When he saw me at last he gave chase. I am afraid he will slay me when he comes."

"I think, perhaps, I may be able to reason with this person when he arrives," said the Professor, rubbing his chin and looking at the hermit over the top of his spectacles. "The Baron ought to be ashamed of himself to go on in this manner! Tilly, wipe the poor creature's eyes with your handkerchief. There now, dear, cheer up."

Just then the Baron rushed into the cell, with his eyes flaming, and his breath coming short and fast.

He was a large man, with a handsome face, thick covered with beard. He was dressed in doublet, trunks and hose, and over one shoulder a mantle hung gracefully. His sword was in its sheath, and it was manifest that he had repented of his murderous purpose.

"Where is that faithless girl?" he demanded in a voice of thunder.

Ysolt had hidden behind Matilda Baffin.

"Say, priest, where have you secreted her?"

"One moment!" said the Professor, stepping forward. "May I, without appearing impertinent, offer a suggestion?"

"Out, varlet!" exclaimed the Baron, pushing him aside. "Tell me, Hermit, where is Ysolt."

The Professor was actually pale with indignation. Pushing himself in front of the Baron, and brandishing his umbrella in a determined way he said:

"Old man, I want you to understand that you have to deal with a free and independent American citizen! What do you mean by 'varlet?' I hurl the opprobrious word back into your teeth, sir! I am not going to put up with such conduct, I'd like you to know!"

The Baron for the first time perceived what manner of man the Professor was, and he paused for a moment amid his rage to eye the stranger with astonishment.

"Why do you want to hurt the young woman? Is this any way for an affectionate father to behave to his own offspring? Allow me to say, sir, that I'll be hanged if I think it is! If you don't want her to marry Sir What's-his-name, don't let her; but it strikes me that charging around the country after her, and threatening to kill her, is an evidence that you don't understand the first principles of domestic discipline!"

"What do you mean? Who are you? What are you doing here?" demanded the Baron, fiercely, recovering his self-possession.

"I am Professor E. L. Baffin, of Wingohocking University; and I mean to try to persuade you to treat your daughter more gently," said the Professor, cooling as he remembered that the Baron had a father's authority.

"You have a weapon. I will fight you," said the Baron, drawing his sword.

The Professor put his cigar in his mouth, and opened his umbrella suddenly in the Baron's face.

The Baron retreated a distance of twenty feet and looked scared.

"Come," said the Professor, closing his umbrella and smiling, "I am not a fighting man. We will not quarrel. Let us talk the matter over calmly."

But the Baron, mortified because of the alarm that he had manifested, rushed savagely at the Professor, and would have felled him to the earth had not Matilda sprung forward and placed herself, shrieking, between the Baron and her father.

At this precise juncture, also, a young man entered the cell, and, seeing the Baron apparently about to strike a woman, seized his sword-arm and held it. The Baron turned sharply about. Recognizing the youth as his son, he simply looked at him angrily, and then, while Miss Baffin clung to the Professor, the Baron seized Ysolt by the arm and led her weeping away.

The Professor, after freeing himself from Miss Baffin's embrace, extended his hand to the youth, and said, —

"I have not the honor of knowing you, sir, but

you have behaved handsomely. Permit me to inquire your name?"

"Sir Dinadan; the son of the Baron," said the youth, taking hold of the Professor's hand, as if he were somewhat uncertain what he had better do with it.

"No last name?" asked the Professor.

"That is all. And you are? — "

"I am Everett L. Baffin, a Professor in the Wingohocking University. I was cast ashore down here with my daughter. Tilly, let me introduce to you Sir Dinadan."

Sir Dinadan colored, and dropping upon his knee he seized Miss Baffin's hand and kissed it. Rising, he said:

"What, Sir Baffin, is the name of the sweet lady?"

"Matilda."

"How lovely!" exclaimed Sir Dinadan.

"It is abbreviated sometimes to Tilly, by her friends."

"It is too beautiful," said the youth, gazing at Miss Baffin with unconcealed admiration. "I trust, Sir Baffin, I may be able to serve in some manner you and the Lady Tilly."

"Professor Baffin, my dear sir; not Sir Baffin. Permit me to offer you my card."

Sir Dinadan took the card, and seemed perplexed as to its meaning. He turned it over and over in a despairing sort of way in his fingers.

"If you will read it," said the Professor, "you will find my name upon it."

"But, Sir Baffin, I cannot read."

"Can't read!" exclaimed the Professor, in amazement. "You don't mean to say that you have never learned to read!"

"High-born people," replied Sir Dinadan, with an air of indifference, "care nothing for learning. We leave that to the monks."

"This," said the Professor to Miss Baffin, "is one of the most extraordinary circumstances that has yet come under my observation. Tilly, mention in your journal that the members of the upper classes are wholly illiterate."

"As the Lady Tilly is a stranger here," said Sir Dinadan, "I would be glad to have her walk with me to the brow of the hill. I will show her our beautiful park."

"That would be splendid!" said Miss Baffin. "May I go, pa?"

"Well, I don't know," said the Professor, with hesitation, and looking inquiringly at the Hermit. As that individual appeared to regard the proposition with no such feeling of alarm as would indicate a breach of ordinary social custom, the Professor continued, "Yes, dear, but be sure not to go beyond ear-shot."

Sir Dinadan, smiling, led Miss Baffin away, and the Professor sat down to finish his cigar and to have some further conversation with the Hermit. Before he had time to begin, two other visitors arrived. Both were young men, gaily dressed in rich costume. One of them, whom the recluse greeted as Sir Bleoberis, had a tall slender figure and an exceedingly handsome countenance, which was adorned with a moustache and pointed beard. His companion, Sir Agravaine, was smaller, less comely, and if his face was an index of his mind, by no means so intelligent.

After being presented to the Professor, whom they regarded with not a little curiosity, Sir Bleoberis said:

"Holy father, the fair Ysolt was here and was taken away by the Baron, was she not?"

"Yes!"

"Alas!" said the Knight, "I see no hope. Whilst I am poor, the Baron will never relent."

"Never!" chimed in Sir Agravaine.

"Is your poverty the only objection he has to you?" asked the Professor.

"Yes."

"Well," replied the Professor, "I can understand a father's feelings in such a case. It seems hard upon a young man, but naturally he wants his daughter to be comfortable. Is there nothing you can turn your hand to to improve your fortunes?"

"We might rob somebody," said Sir Agravaine, with a reflective air.

"Rob somebody!" exclaimed the Professor, "That is simply atrocious! Can't you go to work; go into business, start a factory, speculate in stocks, or something of that kind?"

"Persons of my degree never work," said Sir Bleoberis.

The Professor sighed, "Ah! I forgot. We must think of something else. Let me see; young man, I think I can help you a little, perhaps. You agree to accept some information from me and I believe I can make your fortune."

"Do you propose," asked Sir Agravaine, "to drug the Baron, or to enchant him so that he will change his mind? I have often tried love-philters with ladies whose hands I sought, but they always failed."

"Nonsense!" exclaimed the Professor. "I don't operate with such trumpery as that. You agree to help me, and we'll give this island such a stirring up as will revolutionize it."

The Professor then proceeded to explain in detail the nature and operation of some of the scientific apparatus which he had with him in his trunk; and the Knight and the Hermit listened with open-eyed amazement while he told them of the telegraph, the telephone, the phonograph, the photograph, and other modern inventions.

Whilst the Professor waxed eloquent, Sir Dinadan and Miss Baffin strolled slowly back towards the cave.

Sir Dinadan had improved the opportunity to offer Miss Baffin his hand, rather abruptly.

"But you can try to love me," he pleaded, as she, with much embarrassment but with gentleness, resisted his importunity.

"I can try, Sir Dinadan," she said, blushing, "but really I have known you only a few moments. It is impossible for me now to have any affection for you."

"Will to-morrow be time enough?"

"No, no! I must have a much longer time than that."

"I will fight for you. We will get up a tournament and you will see how I can unhorse the bravest knights. If I knock over ten, will that make any difference in your feelings?"

"Not the slightest!"

"Fifteen?"

"You do not understand. It is not the custom in our country to press a suit upon a lady by poking people off of a horse."

"Perhaps I ought to fight your father? Will Sir Baffin break a lance with me to decide if I shall have you?"

"My father does not fight."

"Does not fight! Certainly you don't mean that?"

"He is the Vice-President of the Universal Peace Society."

"The WHAT?" asked Sir Dinadan, in amazement.

"Of the Peace Society; a society which opposes fighting of every kind, under any circumstances."

It was a moment or two before Sir Dinadan could get his breath. Then he said —

"But — but then, Lady Tilly, what — what do men in your country do with themselves?"

Miss Baffin laughed and endeavored to explain to him the modern methods of existence.

"I never could have believed such a thing from other lips," said Sir Dinadan. "It is marvellous. But tell me, how do lovers woo in your land?"

"Really, Sir Dinadan," replied Miss Baffin, blushing, "I have had no experience worth speaking of in such matters. I suppose, perhaps, they show a lady that they love her, and then wait until she can make up her mind."

"I will wait, then, as long as you wish."

"But," said Miss Baffin, shyly, although plainly she was beginning to feel a genuine interest in the proceeding, "your father and your mother may not think as you do; and then, I shall not want to stay upon this island if I can get away."

"My mother always consents to anything I wish, and the Baron never dares to oppose what she wants. And if you go back to your own country, I will go with you, whether you accept me or not."

Miss Baffin smiled. Sir Dinadan was in earnest, at any rate. She could not help thinking of the sensation that would be created in Wingohocking if she should walk up the fashionable street of the town some afternoon with Sir Dinadan in his particolored dress of doublet and stockings, and jaunty feathered cap, and sword, while his long yellow hair dangled about his shoulders.

While Sir Dinadan was protesting that he should love her for ever and for ever, they came back again to the Hermit's cell, and then Sir Dinadan, greeting Sir Bleoberis and Sir Agravaine, presented Miss Baffin to them.

Sir Bleoberis was courteous but somewhat indifferent; Sir Agravaine, upon the contrary, appeared to be deeply impressed with Miss Baffin's beauty. After gazing at her steadily for a few moments, he approached her, and while the other members of the company engaged in conversation, he said, —

"Fair lady, you are not married?"

"No, sir," replied Miss Baffin, with some indignation.

"Permit me, then, to offer you my hand."

"What!" exclaimed Miss Baffin, becoming angry.

"I love you. Will you be mine?" said Sir Agravaine, falling upon one knee and trying to take her hand.

Miss Baffin boxed his ear with a degree of violence.

Rising with a rueful countenance, he said, —

"Am I to understand, then, that you decline the offer?"

Miss Baffin, without replying, walked away from him and joined her father.

Sir Dinadan was asking the Hermit for a few simples with which to relieve the suffering of his noble mother.

"I judge, from what you say," remarked the Professor, "that the Baroness is afflicted with lumbago. The Hermit's remedies, I fear, will be ineffectual. Permit me to recommend you to iron her noble back, and to apply a porous plaster."

Sir Dinadan wished to have the process more clearly explained. The Professor unfolded the matter in detail, and said, —

"I have some plasters in my trunk, down there upon the beach."

"Then you are a leech?" asked Sir Dinadan.

"Matilda, my child," remarked the Professor, "observe that word 'leech' used by Sir Dinadan! How very interesting it is! Not exactly a leech, Sir Dinadan; but it is my habit to try to know a little of everything."

"Can you cast a lover's horoscope?" asked Sir Agravaine, looking at Matilda.

"Young man," said the Professor, sternly, "there is no such foolery as a horoscope; and as for love, you had better let it alone until you have more wit and a heavier purse."

"I wish you and the Lady Tilly to come with me to the castle," remarked Sir Dinadan. "My father will welcome you heartily if you can medicine the sickness of my mother; and she will be eager to receive your fair daughter."

"I will go, of course," replied the Professor; "you are very kind. Tilly, we had better accept, I think?"

Miss Baffin was willing to leave the matter wholly in the hands of her father.

After requesting Sir Dinadan to have his luggage brought up from the beach, the Professor bade adieu to the Hermit, and then turning to Sir Bleoberis, who stood with a disconsolate air by the fire, he said:

"I will see you again about your affair; and meantime you may depend upon my using my influence with the Baron to remove his prejudices. I will dance at your wedding yet; that is, figuratively speaking, of course; for, as a precise matter of fact, I do not know how to dance."

As the Professor and Sir Dinadan and Miss Baffin left the cell, Sir Agravaine approached the lady and whispered:

"Did I understand you to say you don't love me?"

Miss Baffin twitched the skirt of her gown to one side in a scornful way, and passed on without replying.

"Women," sighed Sir Agravaine, as he looked mournfully after her, " are *so* incomprehensible. I wish I knew what she meant."

CHAPTER II.

THE CASTLE OF BARON BORS.

AS Sir Dinadan led the Professor and Miss Baffin along the lovely path which went winding through the woods toward the castle, the Professor lighted another cigar, and in response to Sir Dinadan, he entered upon an explanation of the nature of tobacco, the methods and extent of its use, and its effect upon the human system.

"The Lady Tilly, of course she smokes sometimes, also?" asked Sir Dinadan.

"Oh, no," replied Miss Baffin, "ladies in my country never do."

"Of course not," added the Professor.

"And yet, if it is so pleasing and so beneficial as you say," responded the youth, "why should not ladies attempt it?"

The Professor really could not say; Sir Dinadan was pressing him almost too closely. He compromised further discussion by yielding promptly, although with a melancholy reflection that his store of cigars was small, to a request to teach Sir Dinadan, at the earliest opportunity, to smoke.

As they neared the castle, the Professor's attention was absorbed in observing the details of the structure. It was a massive edifice of stone, having severe outlines and no ornamentation worthy of the name, but presenting, from the very grandeur of its proportions, an impressive and not unpleasing appearance. It was surrounded by a wide fosse filled with water; and the Professor was delighted to observe, as they drew near, that the entrance was protected with a portcullis and a drawbridge. The bridge was drawn up, and the iron portcullis, made of bars of huge size, was closed.

"Magnificent, isn't it, Tilly?" exclaimed the Professor, gleefully. "It is probably the most perfect specimen of early English architecture now upon earth. Most fortunately I have in my trunks a photographic apparatus with which to obtain a picture of it."

Sir Dinadan seized a curved horn which hung upon the branch of a tree, and blew a blast loud and long upon it.

The Professor regarded the performance with intense interest and not a little enthusiasm.

The warder of the castle appeared at the grating, and, perceiving Sir Dinadan, saluted him; then lowering the drawbridge and lifting the portcullis, which ascended with many hideous creaks and groans from the rusty iron, Sir Dinadan and his companions entered.

Leaving the Professor and Miss Baffin comfortably seated in a great hall, the walls of which were adorned with curious tapestries dark with age, with swords and axes and trophies of the chase, Sir Dinadan went in search of the Baron.

"Little did we think, Tilly," said the Professor, looking around, "when we left New York four weeks ago — it seems more like four years — that we should find ourselves, within a month, in such a place as this."

"I can hardly believe it yet," responded Miss Baffin.

"It does seem like a dream. And yet we are certainly wide awake, and we are in the hall of a real castle, waiting for real people to come to us."

"Sir Dinadan seems very real, too," said Miss Baffin, timidly.

"Very! There can be no doubt about it."

"And he behaves like a real young man, too," continued Miss Baffin. "He proposed to me this morning."

"What! Proposed to you! Incredible! Why, the boy has not known you more than an hour or two."

"He is a man, pa; not a boy," said Miss Baffin, a little hurt. "It *was* rather sudden; but, then, genuine affection sometimes manifests itself in that way."

The Professor smiled; he perceived the exact situation of things. Then he looked very serious again. This was a contingency of which he had not taken account.

"Well, Tilly," he said, "I hardly know what to say about the matter. It is so completely unexpected. You didn't accept him?"

"No; not exactly, but —"

"Very well, then. We will leave the situation as it is for the present. When we have been here longer we can better determine what we should do."

Sir Dinadan entered with the Baron. The Baron greeted his guests with warmth, making no allusion to the occurrences in the Hermit's cell, and appearing, indeed, to have forgotten them.

"It is enough, sir, and fair damsel, that misfortune has thrown you upon our shores. You shall make this your home while you live."

"A thousand thanks," responded the Professor.

"I cherish the belief that I can be of service to you. By the way, may I ask how is the noble Lady Bors?"

"Suffering greatly. My son tells me you are a wise leech, and can give her release from her pain."

"I hope I can. If you will permit my daughter, here, to see the lady and to follow my directions, we may be able to help her."

"There," said the Baron, waving his hand, "are your apartments. When you have made ready we will summon you to our banquet."

"Your property, which was upon the beach, will be placed before you very soon," said Sir Dinadan.

The Professor and Miss Baffin entered the rooms, and the Baron withdrew with his son.

When the trunks came and were opened, the guests arrayed themselves in their finest costumes, and Miss Baffin contrived to give to her beauty a bewildering effect by an artistic arrangement of frippery, which received its consummation when she placed some lovely artificial flowers in her hair.

Then the Professor, giving her certain plasters and a soothing drug or two, requested a servant, who stood outside the door, to announce to Lady Bors that Miss Baffin was ready to give her treatment.

Sir Dinadan came forward and gallantly escorted Miss Baffin to his mother's room; where, after presenting her, he left her and returned to the Professor.

The young man led the Professor about the castle, showing him its apartments, its furniture and decorations, with an earnest purpose to try to find favor in the eyes of the father of the woman he loved. The Professor, for his part, was charmed with his companion, and his interest in the castle and its appurtenances increased every moment.

"This," said Sir Dinadan, pausing before a large oaken door, barred with iron, "is the portal to the upper room of the south tower. In this chamber the Baron has confined Ysolt, my sister, until she consents to think no more of Sir Bleoberis."

"Locked her up, has he? That seems hard."

"Cruel, is it not?"

"You favor the suit of the Knight, do you?" inquired the Professor.

"I would let Ysolt choose for herself. He is a worthy man; but he has poverty."

"We must try to help him," said the Professor.

"You would act differently in such a case; would you not?" asked Sir Dinadan, rather eagerly.

"Why, yes, of course; that is, I mean," said the Professor, suddenly recollecting himself, and what Miss Baffin had told him, "I mean, I would think about it. I would give the matter thoughtful consideration."

Sir Dinadan sighed, and asked the Professor if he would come with him to the dining-hall.

It was a noble room. As the Professor entered it with Sir Dinadan, as he looked at the vast fireplace filled with burning logs, because the air of the castle was chilly even in summer time, at the rudely carved beams that traversed the ceiling, at the quaint curtains and curious ornaments upon the walls, at the long table which stretched across the floor and bore upon its polished surface a multitude of vessels of strange and often fantastic shapes, he could hardly believe his senses. These things, this method of existence, he had read about myriads of times, but they had never seemed very real to him until he encountered them here face to face.

These people among whom he had come by such strange mischance actually lived and moved here, amid these scenes, and they were as common and as prosy to them as the scenes in his own home in the little enclosure hard by the walls of the university building at Wingohocking.

It was that home and its equipment that seemed strange and incongruous to him now. As he thought about it, he felt that he would experience an actual nervous shock if he should suddenly be plumped down in his own library. Very oddly, as his mind reverted to the subject, his memory recalled with peculiarly vivid distinctness an old and faded dressing-gown in which he used to come to breakfast ; and a blue cream-jug with a broken handle, which used to be placed before him at the meal.

It seemed to him that the dressing-gown and the defective jug were as far back in the misty past as such a social condition as that with which he had now been brought into contact would have seemed if he had thought of it a month ago.

As the servants entered, bearing the viands upon

large dishes, the Baron made his appearance at the upper end of the room, and a moment later Lady Bors walked slowly in, leaning upon the arm of Miss Baffin.

"Your sweet daughter," she said, when the Professor had been presented to her, "has eased my pain already. I think she must be an angel sent to me by Heaven."

"She *is* an angel," said Sir Dinadan, emphatically, so that his mother looked at him curiously. Miss Baffin blushed.

"Angels, my lady, do not come with porous plasters," said the Professor, smiling.

"I love her already, whether she is angel or woman," replied Lady Bors, patting Miss Baffin's arm.

"So do —," Sir Dinadan did not complete the sentence. It occurred to him that he might perhaps be getting a little too demonstrative.

"The Lady Tilly," said the Baroness, "has told me something of the adventure which brought you here. Will you be so courteous as to tell us more, and to inform us of that strange and wonderful land from which you have come?"

"Willingly, madam," replied the Professor. And so, while the meal was in progress, the Professor, — not neglecting the food, for he was really hungry, — tried, in the plainest language he could command, to convey to the minds of his hearers some notion of the marvels of modern civilization. The Baron, Lady Bors, and Sir Dinadan asked many questions, and they more than once expressed the greatest astonishment at the revelations made in the Professor's narrative.

"I will show you some of these wonders," said Professor Baffin. "Most happily I have with me in my trunks quite a number of instruments, such as those I have told you of."

"In your trunks!" exclaimed the Baron. "You do not wear trunks, as we do."

The Professor at once explained the misapprehension. When he had done, there was heard in the room the twanging of the strings of a rude musical instrument.

"It is the minstrel," said Sir Dinadan, as the Professor and Miss Baffin looked around.

The Professor was delighted.

"He is going to sing," said the Baron.

The bard, after a few preliminary thrums upon an imbecile harp, burst into song. He occupied several moments in reciting a ballad of chivalry, and although his manner was dramatic, his voice was sadly cracked and out of tune.

"Tilly," said the Professor, "remember to note in your journal that the musical system here is constructed from a defective minor scale, with incorrect intervals. I observed precisely the same characteristics in the song that our Irish nurse,

Mary, used to put you to sleep with when you were a baby. I stood outside the chamber door one night, and wrote the strain down as she sang it. This proves that it is very ancient."

"You like the song, then?" asked the Baron.

"It is very interesting, indeed — very!" replied the Professor. "I think we shall obtain a great deal of valuable information here. No, Tilly, you had better refuse it," said the Professor, observing that Sir Dinadan, who appeared to be animated by a resolute purpose to stuff Miss Baffin, was pressing another dish upon her, "you will spoil your night's rest."

"Do you sing, Sir Baffin?" inquired Lady Bors.

"Never in company, my lady," replied the Professor; "my vocalization would excite too much alarm."

The Baron and his wife manifestly did not comprehend the pleasantry.

"My daughter sings very nicely; but you can hear her sing without her lips being opened. Excuse me for a moment."

The Professor went to his apartment, and presently returned, bringing with him a phonograph. Placing it upon the table, he turned the crank. From the funnel at once issued a lovely soprano voice, singing, with exquisite enunciation and inflection, a song, every word of which was heard by the listeners.

THE CASTLE OF BARON BORS. 57

Lady Bors looked scared, Sir Dinadan crossed himself, the Baron eyed the Professor doubtfully, the minstrel over in the corner laid down his harp, and relieved his overcharged feelings by bursting into tears, which he wiped away with the sleeve of his tunic.

"It must be magic," said the Baron, at last; "no mere man could hide an angelic spirit in such a place, and compel it to sing."

"Allow me to explain," said the Professor; and then he unfolded the mechanism, and showed the method of its operation. "My daughter sang up several songs for me before we left home. They were stored away here for future use. Tilly, my love, sing something, so that our friends can perceive that it is the same voice."

Miss Baffin, after some hesitation, began "The Last Rose of Summer." While she sang, Sir Dinadan looked at her with rapture depicted on his countenance. When she had done he reflected for an instant, and then, rising and walking over to the place where the minstrel sat, he seized by the ear that unfortunate operator with defective minor scales, and, leading him to the door, he kicked him into the hall.

This appeared to relieve Sir Dinadan's feelings.

When he returned, the Professor persuaded him to have his voice recorded by the phonograph; and by the time the Baron and Lady Bors had also tried the experiment, the faith of the family in the powers of Professor Baffin had risen to such a pitch that the Baron would have been almost ready to lay wagers in favor of his omnipotence.

The Professor that evening accepted for himself and his daughter a very urgent invitation to make the castle their home, at least until Fate and the future should determine if they were to remain permanently upon the island. The chance that they would ever escape seemed indeed, exceedingly slender; and the Professor resolved to accept the promise with philosophical resignation.

He employed much of his time during the first weeks that he was the Baron's guest in making the Baron familiar with some of the wonders of modern discovery and invention. The Baron also was deeply interested in an exhibition given by the Professor of the powers of his patent india-rubber life-raft, which the Professor brought up from the beach folded into a small bundle. After inflating it, to the amazement of the spectators, he put it into the fosse that surrounded the castle and paddled about upon it. The raft was allowed to remain in the ditch ready for use.

The Professor often went outside the castle walls to talk with Sir Bleoberis, and to comfort him. The Professor explained the telegraph and the locomotive to the Knight; and when the Knight assured him that the armorers of the island could make the machinery that would be required, if they should receive suitable instructions, the Professor arranged to build a short railroad line and a telegraph line in partnership with Sir Bleoberis, if the latter would obtain the necessary concession from King Brandegore. Professor Baffin was of the opinion that the Knight, by such means, might ultimately acquire great wealth.

Meantime Sir Dagonet had been seen several times of late in the vicinity of the castle, and once he had made again a formal demand upon the Baron for Ysolt's hand. This the Baron refused, whereupon Sir Dagonet returned an insolent reply that he would have her in spite of her father's objection. The Professor sincerely pitied both Ysolt and Sir Bleoberis, but as the Baron always became violently angry when the suffering of the lovers was alluded to, the Professor disliked to plead their cause.

It occurred to him, however, one day that there could be no possible harm in arranging to permit the forlorn creatures to converse with each other; and so, with the help of Miss Baffin, who was allowed to enter the captive's room, he fixed up a telephone, the machinery of which he had in one of his trunks, with a wire running from Ysolt's window to a point some distance beyond the castle wall.

The battery with which the instruments were

supplied was placed in an iron box furnished by Sir Bleoberis, and hidden behind a huge oak tree.

The lovers were delighted with the telephone and its performances; but the Professor's ingenious kindness caused him a great deal of serious trouble.

It seems that Miss Baffin one morning had been showing her father's umbrella to Ysolt, and making her acquainted with its peculiarities and uses.

When Miss Baffin had withdrawn, Sir Bleoberis began to breathe through the telephone protestations of his undying love, and finally he appealed to Ysolt to fly with him. Of course he expected nothing to come of this appeal, for he had not the slightest conception of any method by which Ysolt could escape from her prison. He merely threw it in, in a general sort of a way, as an expression of the intensity of his affection.

But it suggested to the mind of Ysolt an ingenious thought; and she responded through the telephone that if Sir Bleoberis would keep out of sight and have his gallant steed ready, she would join him in a few moments. The Knight's heart beat so fiercely at this news that it fairly made his armor vibrate.

Obeying the orders of Ysolt, he went behind the oak and sat upon the iron box containing the Professor's battery and electrical apparatus.

Ysolt's window was but twenty feet from the surface of the water in the fosse. Directly beneath it,

WHY SIR BLEOBERIS DID NOT LEAP TO THE RESCUE.   Page 61.

by a most fortunate chance, floated the life-raft of Professor Baffin. The brave girl, climbing upon the stone sill of the window, hoisted the umbrella, and sailing swiftly downward through the air, she alighted safely upon the raft. A single push upon the wall sent it to the further side of the ditch, whereupon Ysolt leaped ashore, unperceived by the warder or by any one in the castle.

A moment more, and seated upon the steed of her cavalier, with his strong arm around her, she would be flying to peace and happiness and love's sweet fulfilment, far, far beyond the reach of the angry Baron's power.

But, alas, human life is so full of mischances! As Ysolt neared the great oak behind which her lover sat, Sir Dagonet came riding carelessly across the lawn. Seeing her he spurred his horse forward, and, right before the eyes of Sir Bleoberis, he grasped her by the arm, tossed her to his saddle and dashed away across the country.

But why did not Sir Bleoberis leap to the rescue?

Sir Bleoberis tried with all his might to do so; but he had on a full suit of steel armor, and the Professor's battery, by some means even yet unexplained, so charged the cover of the box with magnetism that it held the Knight close down. He could not move a muscle of his legs. He writhed and twisted and expressed his fury in language that was vehement and scandalous; but the Professor's infamous machine held him fast ; and he was compelled to sit by, imbecile and raging, while the wind bore to his ears the heart-rending screams of his sweetheart as she cried to him to come and save her from an awful fate.

The shrieks of the unhappy Ysolt penetrated to the castle, and at once the Baron ran out, followed by Sir Dinadan, Professor Baffin, and a host of the Baron's retainers, all of them armed and ready for war. The first act of the Professor was to capture his expanded umbrella, which was being blown about wildly by the wind. Furling it, he proceeded to the place where Sir Bleoberis sat, trying to explain to the infuriated Baron what had happened.

"There!" said Sir Bleoberis, savagely, pointing to the Professor, "is the vile wretch that did it all! Seize him! He, he alone is to blame."

The Professor was amazed.

"Yes!" exclaimed Sir Bleoberis, "it was he who persuaded the fair Ysolt to leap from the window; it was he who notified Sir Dagonet, and it is his wicked enchantment that held me here so that I could not fly to her succor. I cannot even get up now."

"The man," said the Professor to the Baron, "appears to be suffering from intellectual aberration. I can't imagine what he means. Why don't you rise?"

THE CASTLE OF BARON BORS.

"You, foul wizard, know that I am held here by your infernal power!"

"Try to be calm," said the Professor, soothingly.. "Your expressions are too strong. Let me see —. Why, bless my soul, the electrical current has magnetized the box. There, now," said the Professor as he snipped a couple of the wires, "try it again."

Sir Bleoberis arose without effort. Baron Bors stepped forward and said sternly:

"What, you, Sir Bleoberis, were doing here I do not know. I suspect you of evil purposes. But it is clear you had nothing to do with the seizure of my daughter, if, indeed, she has been carried off by Sir Dagonet. You may go. But as for you," shouted the Baron, turning to the Professor, "I perceive that your devilish arts have been used against me and my family while you have been eating my bread. The world shall no longer be burdened by such a monster. Away with him to the scaffold!"

"This," said the Professor, as the perspiration stood in beads upon his pallid face, "is painful; very painful. Allow me to explain. The fact is I—"

"Away!" said the Baron, with an impatient gesture. "Off with his head as quickly as possible!"

"But, my dear sir," contended the Professor, as the Baron's retainers seized him, "this is simply awful! No court, no jury, no trial, no chance to tell my story! It is not just. It is not fair play. Permit me, for one moment, to —"

"To the block with him!" screamed the Baron. "Have no more parley about it!"

Sir Bleoberis came forward.

"Sir Bors," he said, "this, in a measure, is my quarrel. It falls to me by right to punish this wretch. Will you permit me?" and then Sir Bleoberis struck the Professor in the face with his mailed gauntlet.

Professor Baffin would have assailed him upon the spot, but for the fact that he was a captive.

"He means that you shall fight him," said Sir Dinadan, who retained his faith in the Professor, remembering his own affection for Miss Baffin.

"Certainly I will," said the Professor. "Where, and when, and how? I would like to have it out right here on the spot."

It is melancholy to think what would have been the sorrow of the members of the Universal Peace Society, of which the Professor was the first vice-president, if they could have observed the eagerness with which that good man seemed to long for the fray, and the fiery rage which beamed from his eyes until the sparks almost appeared to fly from his spectacles.

Miss Baffin at this moment rushed upon the scene, and in wild affright flung her arms about her father.

"The contest shall be made," said the Baron, sternly. "Unhand him!"

The Professor hurriedly explained the matter to Matilda, who sobbed piteously.

"You shall have my armor, my horse, and my lance," said Sir Dinadan in a kindly voice to the Professor. "Go and get them," he continued, speaking to some of the servants.

"Thank you," said the Professor. "I am much obliged. You are a fine young man."

"But, pa," said Miss Baffin through her tears, "surely you are not going to fight.?"

"Yes, my love."

"And you a member of the Peace Society, too."

"I can't help it, my child. You may omit to note this extraordinary occurrence in your journal. The Society may as well remain in ignorance of it. But I must conform to the customs of the place."

"How can you ever do anything upon a horse, with armor and a lance? It is dreadful!"

"No, my child, it may perhaps be regarded as fortunate. For many years I have longed to observe the practices of ancient chivalry more closely; that opportunity has now come. I am about to have actual practical experience with them."

Miss Baffin wiped her eyes as Sir Dinadan came to her side and tried to comfort her. Sir Agravaine, who had ridden up during the excitement, dismounted when he saw Miss Baffin, and pulling Sir Dinadan by the sleeve, he whispered :

" You are acquainted with that lady ? "

" Yes."

" Would you mind ascertaining for me if I am to understand her remarkable conduct to me as tantamount to a refusal ? I don't want to trouble you, but —"

Sir Dinadan turned abruptly away, leaving Sir Agravaine still involved in doubt.

When the armor came, Sir Dinadan helped the Professor to put it on. It was a size or two too large for him, and the Professor had a considerable amount of difficulty in adjusting the pieces properly, but, with the help of Sir Dinadan, he at last succeeded.

" Bring me my lance ! " he exclaimed, with a firm voice, as he stepped forward.

" It is here," said Sir Dinadan.

" Farewell, my child," said the Professor to Miss Baffin, making a futile attempt to bend his elbows so that he could embrace her. " Farewell ! " and the Professor tried to kiss her, but he merely succeeded in injuring her nose with the visor of his helmet.

" O pa ! " said Miss Baffin, weeping, " if you should be killed."

" No danger of that love, none at all. I am perfectly safe. I feel exactly as if I were a cooking-stove, to be sure; but you may depend upon my giving a good account of myself. And now, dear, adieu! Ho, there!" exclaimed the Professor, with faint reminiscences of the tragic stage coming into his mind. "Bring me my steed!"

The determined efforts of four muscular men were required to mount the Professor upon his horse. And when he was fairly astride, with his lance in his hand, he felt as if he weighed at least three thousand pounds, and the weapon seemed quite as large as the jib-boom of the "Morning Star."

The warrior did his best to sit his horse gracefully; but the miserable beast pranced and curveted in such a very unreasonable manner that his spectacles were continually shaking loose, and in his efforts to fix them, and at the same time to hold his horse, he lost control of his lance, and came near impaling two or three of the spectators.

Sir Dinadan's own groom then took the bridle-rein, and leading the horse quietly to the jousting-ground put him in place directly opposite to Sir Bleoberis, whose lance was in rest, and who evidently intended to spit the Professor through and through at the first encounter.

The Professor really felt uncomfortably at a disadvantage in his iron-clad condition, and he began to think that the sports and combats of the olden time were perhaps not so interesting after all, when brought within the range of practical experience.

Suddenly the herald's trumpet sounded a blast. The Professor had not the least notion of the meaning of the sound, but Sir Bleoberis started promptly towards him, and the Professor's horse, trained at jousting, also started. The Professor was not quite ready, and he pulled the rein hard while trying to fix his lance in its rest. This caused the horse to swerve sharply around, whereupon the warrior's spectacles came off, and the horse dashed at full speed to the side of the jousting-ground, bringing the half-blinded Professor's lance up against a tree, into which the point stuck fast. The Professor was hurled with some violence to the ground, and the horse ran away.

When they picked him up and unlatched his helmet, he was bleeding at the nose.

"It is of no consequence, Matilda, of no consequence, I assure you," he said. "I am shaken up a little, but not hurt. I think, perhaps, I need practice at this kind of thing."

The Professor, while speaking, felt about him in a bewildered way for the pocket in which he was used to keep his handkerchief. But as the armor baffled his efforts to find it, Miss Baffin offered him her kerchief with which to stanch the blood.

"The ancients, Matilda," said the Professor, as he pressed the handkerchief to his nose, "must have possessed great physical strength, and they could not have been near sighted. By the way, where are my glasses?"

Sir Dinadan handed them to him.

"You will not attempt to get on that horrid horse, again, pa, will you?" said Miss Baffin, entreatingly.

"I think not, my child, unless I am forced to do so. Jousting is interesting to read about; but as a matter of fact it is brutal. I think, Sir Dinadan, I should be more comfortable if I could get this cast-iron overcoat off, so that I could move my elbows without creaking."

Sir Dinadan helped him to remove his armor, and said:

"My noble mother has insisted that Sir Bleoberis shall not fight with you, and the Baron has yielded to her wish."

"How can I thank you?" exclaimed Miss Baffin.

Sir Dinadan looked at her as if he would like to tell her how, if he dared venture. But he only said:

"I deserve no thanks. My mother is upon your side and that of your father. She asks me to bring him to her."

The Baron was with his wife, and Sir Bleoberis stood before them.

"Sir Bamn," said the Baron, "Lady Bors insists

that you are innocent of any wrong-doing; and Sir Bleoberis, seeing that you are unskilled, has resolved not to have a combat with you. I am willing to pardon you upon one condition: that you find my daughter and bring her back to me."

"That I should be willing to try to do under any circumstances," said the Professor. "I regret her loss very deeply. But, you see, I know nothing of the country. I am afraid I should not discover her if I should go alone."

"I will go with you," said Sir Bleoberis.

"That is first-rate," said the Professor. "Give me your hand."

"We will keep your daughter in the castle as a hostage," said the Baron. "When you return with Ysolt you shall have the Lady Tilly, and Sir Bleoberis shall have Ysolt."

"I am profoundly grateful," replied Sir Bleoberis, bowing.

"My dear," said the Professor to Miss Baffin, "does the arrangement suit you?"

"It suits me," muttered Sir Dinadan.

"I must stay whether I wish to or not," replied Miss Baffin. "But I shall worry about you every moment while you are gone."

"Sir Dinadan may be able to soothe her," said Sir Bleoberis, with a smile.

"I think I could, if I were allowed to try," insinuated Sir Agravaine.

"I charge Sir Dinadan and his noble parents with the task," said the Professor.

The entire party, with the exception of Sir Agravaine, then returned to the castle, so that the Professor could make ready for the journey.

CHAPTER III.

THE RESCUE.

PROFESSOR BAFFIN politely declined to wear the armor of Sir Dinadan upon the journey. He packed a few things in a satchel, and putting his revolver in his pocket, he bade adieu to his daughter and the members of the Baron's family. Mounting his horse by the side of Sir Bleoberis, who rode in full armor, the two trotted briskly out through the woods to the roadway, which ran by not far from the castle.

"Where shall we go to look for the lady?" asked the Professor, as the Knight started down the road at a rapid pace.

"The villain, no doubt, has carried her captive to his castle. We shall seek her there."

"How are we going to get her out? I have had very little experience, personally, in storming castles."

"We shall have to devise some plan when we get there," replied the Knight. "The castle, unhappily, is upon an island in the middle of the lake."

"And I can't swim," said the Professor.

"Perhaps the King will give us help. It is close to the place where he holds his court."

The Professor began to think that the case looked exceedingly unpromising. He lapsed into silence, thinking over the probable results of the failure of his mission; and as the Knight appeared to be absorbed in his own reflections, the pair rode forward without engaging in further conversation.

Professor Baffin did not fail to notice the extreme loveliness of the country through which they were passing. It presented all the characteristics of a perfect English landscape; but he observed that it was not fully cultivated, and that the agricultural methods employed were of a very primitive kind.

After an hour's ride, the two horsemen entered a wood. Hardly had they done so before they heard, near to them, the voice of a woman crying loudly for help. Sir Bleoberis at once spurred his horse forward, and the Professor followed close behind him.

Presently they perceived a Knight in armor endeavoring to hold upon the horse in front of him a young woman of handsome appearance, who screamed loudly as she attempted to release herself from his grasp.

"Drop her!" exclaimed the Professor in an excited manner, and drawing his revolver, "put her down; let her go at once!"

The Knight turned, and seeing the intruders he released the maiden, and levelling his lance, made straight for Sir Bleoberis at full gallop.

The lady, white with terror, flew to the Professor, and reposed her head upon his bosom.

Professor Baffin was embarrassed. He had no idea what he had better do or say. He could not repulse the poor creature; and as the situation, upon the whole, was not positively disagreeable, he permitted her to remain, sobbing upon his bosom, while he watched the fight and dried her eyes, in a fatherly way, with his handkerchief.

The two Knights came together with a terrible shock which made the sparks fly; but neither was unhorsed or injured, and the lances of both glanced aside. They turned, and made at each other again. This time the lance of each pierced the armor of the other, so that neither lance could be withdrawn. It really seemed as if the two knights would have to undress and to walk off, leaving their armor pinioned together. A moment later the strange Knight fell to the ground, and lay perfectly still. The Professor went up to him and taking his lance from his hand, so that Sir Bleoberis could move, unlaced the Knight's helmet.

He was dead.

The Professor was inexpressibly shocked.

"Why," he exclaimed, "the man is dead! Most horrible, isn't it?"

"Oh, no," said Sir Bleoberis, coolly. "I tried to kill him."

"You wanted to murder him?"

"Oh, yes, of course."

"I am so glad you did," exclaimed the damsel with a sweet smile. "How can I thank you? And you, my dear preserver."

"Bless my soul, madam," exclaimed the Professor, "I had nothing to do with it. I consider it perfectly horrible."

Turning to Sir Bleoberis, the maiden said, "It was you who fought, but it was this brave and wise man who brought you here, was it not?"

"Yes," said Sir Bleoberis, smiling.

"I knew it," exclaimed the lady, flinging her arms around the Professor's neck. "I can never repay you — never, never, excepting with a life of devotion."

The Professor began to feel warm. Disengaging himself as speedily as possible, he said —

"Of course madam, I am very glad you have been rescued — very. But I deeply regret that the Knight over there was slain. What," asked the Professor of Sir Bleoberis, "will you do with him?"

"Let him lie. He is of no further use."

"I never heard of anything so shocking," said Professor Baffin. "And how are we to dispose of this lady?"

"I will go with you," exclaimed the damsel, looking eagerly at the Professor. "Let me tell you my story. My name is Bragwaine. I am the daughter of the Prince Sagramor. That dead Knight found me, a few hours ago, walking in the park by my father's castle. Sir Lamorak, he was called. Riding up swiftly to me, he seized me, and carried me away. He brought me, despite my screams and struggles, to this place, where you found us both. I should now be a captive in his castle but for you."

Bragwaine seemed about to fall upon the Professor's neck again, but he pretended to stumble, and retreated to a safe distance.

"Is there much of this kind of thing going on,— this business of galloping off with marriageable girls?" asked the Professor.

"Oh yes," said Sir Bleoberis.

"I thought so," said the Professor; "this is the second case I have encountered to-day. We shall most likely have quite a collection of rescued damsels on our hands by the time we get back home. It is interesting, but embarrassing."

"I know Prince Sagramor," said Sir Bleoberis to Bragwaine. "We are going to the court, and will take you to your father."

"*You* will take me, Sir—Sir—"

"Sir Baffin," explained Sir Bleoberis.

"Sir Baffin, will you not?"

"You can have my horse. I will walk."

"I will ride upon your horse with you, and you shall hold me on," said Bragwaine.

"That is the custom," said Bleoberis.

"But," exclaimed the Professor with an air of distress, "I am not used to riding double. I doubt if I can manage the horse and hold you on at the same time."

"You need not hold me," said Bragwaine laughingly; "I will hold fast to you. I shall not fall."

"But then—"

"I *will* go with you," said Bragwaine almost tearfully. "You won me from the hands of that villain, Lamorak, and I am not so ungrateful as to leave you to cling to another person."

"Well, I declare!" exclaimed the Professor, "this certainly is a very curious situation for a man like me to find himself in. However, I will do the best I can."

Professor Baffin mounted his steed, and then Sir Bleoberis swung the fair Bragwaine up to a place on the saddle in front of the Professer. Bragwaine clutched his coat-sleeve tightly; and although the Professor felt that there was no real necessity that she should attempt to preserve her equipoise by pressing his shoulder strongly with her head, he regarded the arrangement without very intense indignation.

He found that he could ride very comfortably

with two in the saddle, but he felt that his attention could be given more effectively to the management of the horse if Bragwaine would stop turning her eyes up to his in that distracting manner so frequently.

They rode along in silence for awhile. Suddenly Bragwaine said:

"Sir Baffin?"

"Well; what?"

"Are you married?"

Professor Baffin hardly knew what answer he had better give. After hesitating for a moment, he said:

"I have been."

"Then your wife is dead?"

The Professor could not lie. He had to say "Yes!"

"I am so glad," murmured Bragwaine. "Not that she is dead, but that you are free."

Professor Baffin was afraid to ask why. He felt that matters were becoming serious.

"And the reason is," continued Bragwaine, "that I have learned to love you better than I love any other one on earth!"

She said this calmly, very modestly, and quite as if it were a matter of course.

The Professor in astonishment looked at Sir Bleoberis, who had heard Bragwaine's words. The Knight nodded to him pleasantly, and said, "I expected this."

Evidently it was not an unusual thing for ladies so to express their feelings.

The somewhat bewildered Sir Baffin then said, "Well, my dear child, it is very kind indeed for you to regard me in that manner. I have done nothing to deserve it."

"You are my rescuer, my benefactor, my heart's idol!"

"Persons at my time of life," said the Professor, blushing, "have to be extremely careful. I will be a father to you, of course! Oh, certainly, you may count upon me being a father to you, right along.'

"I do not mean that I love you as a daughter. You must marry me; you dear Sir Baffin." Then she actually patted his cheek.

Professor Baffin could feel the cold perspiration trickling down his back.

"I think," he said to Sir Bleoberis, "that this is, everything considered, altogether *the* most stupendous combination of circumstances that ever came within the range of my observation. It is positively distressing."

"You will break my heart if you will not love me," said Bragwaine, as if she were going to cry.

"Well, well," replied the bewildered Professor, "we can consider the subject at some other time. Your father, you know, might have other views, and, —"

"The Prince, my father, will overwhelm you

with gratitude for saving me. I know he will approve of our marriage. I will persuade him to have you knighted, and to secure for you some high place at court."

"That," said the Professor, "would probably make me acutely miserable for life."

Within an hour or two after the fight with Sir Lamorak, the Professor and his companions drew near to Callion, the town in which King Brandegore held his court.

Just before entering it they encountered Prince Sagramor coming out with a retinue of knights in pursuit of Sir Lamorak and his daughter. Naturally he was filled with joy at finding that she had been rescued and brought back to him.

After embracing her, he greeted Sir Bleoberis and the Professor warmly, thanking them for the service they had done to him. Bragwaine insisted upon the Professor's especial title to gratitude, and when she had told with eloquence of his wisdom and his valor, and had added to her story Sir Bleoberis's explanation of the Professor's adventures, the Prince saluted the latter, and said:

"There is only one way in which I can honor you, Sir Baffin. I perceive that already you have won the heart of this damsel. I had intended her for another. But she is fairly yours. Take her, gallant sir, and with her a loving father's blessing!"

Bragwaine wept for happiness.

"But, your highness, if I might be permitted to explain —" stammered the Professor.

"I know!" replied the Prince. "You will perhaps say you are poor. It is nothing. I will make you rich. It is enough for me that she loves you, and that you return it."

"I cannot sufficiently thank you for your kindness," said the Professor, "but really there is a —"

"If you are not noble, the King will cure that. He wants such brave men as you are in his service," said the Prince.

"I am a free-born American citizen, and the equal of any man on earth," said the Professor proudly, "but to tell you the honest truth, I —"

"You are not already married?" inquired the Prince, somewhat suspiciously.

"I have been married; my wife is dead, and —"

"Then, of course, you can marry Bragwaine. Sir Colgrevance," said the Prince to one of his attendants, "ride over and tell the abbot that Bragwaine will wish to be married to-morrow!"

"To-morrow!" shrieked the Professor. "I really must protest; you are much too sudden. I have an important mission to fulfil, and I must attend to that first, and at once."

Sir Bleoberis explained to the Prince the nature of their errand, and told him the Professor's daughter was held as a hostage until he should bring Ysolt back to Baron Bors.

"We will delay the wedding, then," said the Prince. "And now, let us ride homeward."

If it had not been for the heart-rending manner in which everybody regarded him as the future husband of Bragwaine, and for the extreme tenderness of that lady's behavior toward him, the Professor would have enjoyed hugely his sojourn at the court. King Brandegore regarded him from the first with high favor, and the sovereign's conduct of course sufficed to recommend the Professor to everybody else. The Professor found the King to be a man of rather large mind, and it was a continual source of pleasure to the learned man to unfold to the King, who listened with amazement and admiration, the wonders of modern invention, science, and discovery.

With what instruments the Professor's ingenuity could construct from the rude materials at hand; he showed a number of experiments, chiefly electrical, which so affected the King that he ordered the regular court magician to be executed as a perfectly hopeless humbug; but Professor Baffin's energetic protest saved the unhappy conjurer from so sad a fate.

An extemporized telegraph line, a few hundred yards in length, impressed the King more strongly than any other thing, and not only did he make to Sir Bleoberis and the Professor exclusive concessions of the right to build lines within his dominions, but he promised to organize, at an early day, a raid upon a neighboring sovereign, for the purpose of obtaining plunder enough to give to the enterprise a handsome subsidy.

Sir Dagonet did not come to court during the Professor's stay. But there, in full view of the palace, a mile away in the lake, was his castle, and in that castle was the lovely Ysolt.

The Professor examined the building frequently through his field-glasses, which, by the way, the King regarded with unspeakable admiration ; and more than once he thought he could distinguish Ysolt sitting by the window of one of the towers overlooking the lake.

The King several times sent to Sir Dagonet messages commanding Sir Dagonet to bring the damsel to him, but as Sir Dagonet invariably responded by trying to brain the messenger or to sink his boat, the King was forced to give it up as a hopeless case. Storming the castle was out of the question. None of the available boats were large enough to carry more than half a dozen men, and Sir Dagonet had many boats of great size which he could man, so as to assail any hostile fleet before it came beneath the castle wall.

But the Professor had a plan of his own, which he was working out in secret, while he waited. Sir Bleoberis had procured several skilful armorers, and under the directions of the Professor they undertook to construct, in rather a crude fashion, a small steam-engine. This, when the parts were completed, was fitted into a boat with a propeller screw, and when the craft was launched upon the lake, the Professor was delighted to find that it worked very nicely. The trial-trip was made at night, so that the secret of the existence of such a vessel might be kept from any of the friends of Sir Dagonet who might be loitering about.

It devolved upon Sir Bleoberis, by bribing a servant of Sir Dagonet's who came ashore, to send a message to Ysolt. She was ordered to watch at a given hour upon a certain night for a signal which should be given from a boat, beneath her window, and then to leap fearlessly into the water.

The night chosen was to be the eve of the Professor's wedding-day. The more Prince Sagramor saw of Professor Baffin and his feats, the more strongly did he admire him; and in order to make provision against any accident which should deprive his daughter of marriage with so remarkable a man, the Prince commanded the wedding-day to be fixed positively, despite the remonstrances which the Professor offered somewhat timidly, in view of the extreme delicacy of the matter.

Upon the night in question, the Professor, at the request of the King, who was very curious to have an opportunity to learn from practical experience the nature of the thing which the Professor called "a lecture," undertook to deliver in the dining-room of the palace the lecture upon Sociology, which he had prepared for his course in England.

The room was packed, and the interest and curiosity at first manifested were intense; but the Professor spoke for an hour and three-quarters, losing his place several times because of the wretched character of the lights, and when he had concluded, he was surprised to discover that his entire audience was sound asleep.

At first he felt rather annoyed, but in an instant he perceived that chance had arranged matters in an extremely favorable manner.

It was within precisely half an hour of the time when he was to be in the boat under the window of Ysolt.

Stepping softly from the platform, he went upon tiptoe from the room. Not a sleeper awoke. Hurrying from the palace to the shore, he found Sir Bleoberis sitting in the boat, and awaiting him with impatience.

The Professor entered the craft, and applying a lighted match to the wood beneath the boiler, he pushed the boat away from the shore, and waited until he could get steam enough to move with.

A few moments sufficed for this, and then, opening the throttle-valve gently, the tiny steamer sailed swiftly over the bosom of the lake, through the intense darkness, until the wall of the castle, dark and gloomy, loomed up directly ahead.

A light was faintly burning in Ysolt's chamber in the tower, and the casement was open.

As the prow of the boat lightly touched the stones of the wall and rested, Sir Bleoberis softly whistled.

"I have always been uncertain," said the Professor to himself, "if the ancients knew how to whistle. This seems to indicate that they did know how. It is extremely interesting. I must remember to tell Tilly to note it in her journal."

In response to the signal, a head appeared at the casement, and a soft, sweet voice said:

"Is that you, darling?"

"Yes, yes, it is I," replied Sir Bleoberis. "Oh, my love! my Ysolt!" he exclaimed, in an ecstasy.

"Is Sir Baffin there, too?"

"Yes. We are both here; and we have a swift boat. Come to me at once, dear love, that we may fly with you homeward."

"I am not quite ready, love," replied Ysolt. "Will not you wait for a moment?"

"It is important," said the Professor, "that we should act quickly."

"But I *must* fix up my hair," returned Ysolt. "I will hurry as much as I can."

"Women," said the Professor to his companion, "are all alike. She would rather remain in prison for life than come out with her hair mussed."

The occupants of the boat waited very impatiently for fifteen or twenty minutes. Then Ysolt, coming again to the window, said:

"Are you there, dearest?"

"Yes," replied Sir Bleoberis, eagerly. "We are all ready."

"And there's no time to lose," added Professor Baffin.

"Is your hair fixed?" asked the Knight.

"Oh, yes," said Ysolt.

"Then come right down."

"Would ten minutes more make any difference?" asked Ysolt.

"It might ruin us," replied the Professor.

"We can wait no longer, darling," said Sir Bleoberis, firmly.

"Then you will have to go without me," said Ysolt, with a tinge of bitterness. "It is simply impossible for me to come till I get my bundle packed."

"We will wait, then," returned Sir Bleoberis, gloomily. Then he said to the Professor: "She had no bundle with her when she was captured."

The Professor, in silent desperation, banked his fires, threw open the furnace-door, and began to wonder what kind of chance he would have in the event of a boiler explosion. Blowing off steam, under the existing circumstances, was simply out of the question.

After a delay of considerable duration, Ysolt's voice was heard again :

" Dearest ! "

" What, love ? " asked Sir Bleoberis.

" I am all ready now," said Ysolt.

" So are we."

" How must I get down ? "

" Climb through the window and jump. You will fall into the water, but I shall catch you and place you in the boat."

" But I shall get horridly wet ! "

" Of course ; but, darling, that can make no great difference, so that you escape."

" And spoil my clothes, too ! "

" Yes, Ysolt, I know ; but — "

" I cannot do it ; I am afraid." And Ysolt began to cry.

Wild despair filled the heart of Sir Bleoberis.

" I have a rope here," said the Professor ; " but how are we to get it up to her ? "

" Ysolt," said Bleoberis, " if I throw you the end of a rope, do you think you can catch it ? "

" I will try."

Sir Bleoberis threw it. He threw it again. He threw it thirteen times, and then Ysolt contrived to catch it.

" What shall I do with it now ? " she asked.

" Tie it fast to something ; to the bed, or anything," replied the Knight.

"Now what shall I do?" asked the maiden, when she had made the rope secure.

"Slide right down into the boat," said the Professor.

"It would ruin my hands," said Ysolt, mournfully.

"Make the attempt, and hold on tightly," said Sir Bleoberis.

"We shall be caught if we stay here much longer," observed the Professor, with anxious thoughts of the boiler.

"Good-bye then! I am lost! Go without me! Save yourselves! Oh, this is terrible!" Ysolt began again to cry.

"I will help her," said Sir Bleoberis, seizing the rope and clambering up the wall until he reached the window.

Day began to dawn as he disappeared in the room. The Professor started his fire afresh and shut the furnace-door. Sir Bleoberis, he knew, would bring down Ysolt without delay.

A moment later, the Knight seated himself upon the stone sill of the window and caught the rope with his feet and one of his hands. Then he placed his arm about Ysolt, lifted her out and began to descend.

Professor Baffin, even in his condition of intense anxiety, could not fail to admire the splendid physical strength of the Knight. When the pair were about half-way down, the rope broke, and Ysolt and Sir Bleoberis were plunged into the lake.

The Professor, excited as he was by the accident, remembered the boiler, and determined that he would have to blow off steam and take the consequences; so he threw open the valve, and instantly the castle walls sent the fierce sound out over the waters.

Sir Bleoberis, with Ysolt upon his arm, managed to swim to the side of the boat, and the Professor after a severe effort lifted her in. Then he gave his hand to the Knight, and as Sir Bleoberis's foot touched the side the Professor shut off steam, opened his throttle-valve, backed the boat away from the wall, and started for the shore.

It was now daylight. As the boat turned the corner of the wall, it almost came into collision with a boat in which, with ten oarsmen, sat Sir Dagonet. The inmates of the castle had been alarmed by the performances of the Professor's escape-pipe; and Sir Dagonet had come out to ascertain the cause of the extraordinary noise.

The Professor's presence of mind was perfect. Turning his boat quickly to the right, he gave the engine a full head of steam and shot away before Sir Dagonet's boat could stop its headway.

Sir Dagonet had perceived Ysolt, and recognized Sir Bleoberis. White with rage he screamed to them to stop, and he hurled at them terrible threats of vengeance if he should overtake them. As no heed was given to him he urged his rowers to put forth their mightiest efforts, and soon his boat was in hot pursuit of that in which the maiden, the Knight, and the Professor fled away from him.

By some means the people of the town of Callion had had their attention drawn to the proceedings at the castle, and now the shore was lined with spectators who watched with eager interest the race between Sir Dagonet's boat and the wonderful craft which had neither oars nor sails, and which sent a long streamer of smoke from out its chimney.

Professor Baffin, positively determined not to wed the daughter of Prince Sagramor, had prepared a stratagem. He had sent three horses to the side of the lake opposite to the town, and three or four miles distant from it, with the intention of landing there, and hurrying with Ysolt and Sir Bleoberis to the home of Baron Bors, without the knowledge of the Prince.

The daylight interfered, to some extent, with the promise of the plan, but Professor Baffin resolved to carry it out at any rate, taking what he considered to be the tolerably good chances of success. He turned the prow of his boat directly toward the town, making as if he would go thither. The pursuers followed fast, and as the Professor perceived that he could easily outstrip them, he slowed his engine somewhat, permitting Sir Dagonet to gain upon him.

When he was within a few hundred yards of the shore, close enough indeed, for him to perceive that the King, Prince Sagramor, Bragwaine, and all the attendants of the court were among those who watched the race with excited interest, the Professor suddenly turned his boat half around, and putting the engine at its highest speed, ploughed swiftly toward the opposite shore.

A mighty shout went up from the onlookers. Manifestly the fugitives had the sympathy of the crowd.

The oarsmen of Sir Dagonet worked right valiantly to win the chase, but the steamer gained constantly upon them; and when her keel grated upon the sand, close by where the horses stood, the pursuers were at least a third of a mile behind.

Sir Bleoberis sprang from the boat, and helped Ysolt to alight. The Professor stopped to make the fire in the furnace more brisk, and to tie down the safety valve; then hurrying after Sir Bleoberis and Ysolt, the three mounted their horses and galloped away.

In a few moments they reached the top of a hill which commanded a view of the lake. They stopped and looked back. Sir Dagonet had just touched the shore, but, as he had no horse, further pursuit was useless. So, shaking his fist at the distant party, he turned away with an affectation of contempt, and entered the Professor's boat to satisfy his curiosity respecting it.

"Let him be careful how he meddles with that," said the Professor.

As he spoke, the boat was torn to fragments. Sir Dagonet and two of his men were seen to fall, and a second afterwards the dull, heavy detonation of an explosion reached the ears of the Professor and his friends.

"It is dreadful," said the Professor with a sigh, "but self-preservation is the first law of nature, and then he had no right to run away with Ysolt, at any rate."

CHAPTER IV.

HOW THE PROFESSOR WENT HOME.

THE three friends turned their horses' heads away from the lake, and pressed swiftly along the road.

"It is necessary," said Professor Baffin, "that we should make good speed, for Prince Sagramor saw us come to this side of the lake, and if he shall suspect our design no doubt he will at once pursue us, in behalf of that abominable girl, his daughter."

The journey was made in silence during most of the time, for the hard riding rendered conversation exceedingly difficult, but whenever the party reached the crest of a hill which commanded a view of the road in the rear, the Professor looked anxiously behind him to ascertain if anybody was giving chase. When within a mile or two of Lonazep, he did at last perceive what appeared to be a group of horsemen at some distance behind him, and although he felt by no means certain that the Prince was among them, he nervously urged his companions forward, spurring, meantime, his own horse furiously, in the hope that he might reach the castle of Baron Bors ere he should be overtaken.

As the party came within sight of the castle, they could hear the hoofs of the horses of the pursuers, and soon their ears were assailed by cries, demanding that they should stop. It was, indeed, Prince Sagramor and his knights, who were following fast. The Professor galloped more furiously than ever when he ascertained the truth, and Sir Bleoberis and Ysolt kept pace with him.

Just as they reached the drawbridge, however, they were overtaken; and, as it was raised, they were compelled to stop and meet the Prince face to face. The Professor hurriedly called to the warder to lower the bridge, so that Ysolt could take refuge in the castle. Then he turned, and determined to make the best of the situation. The Prince was disposed to be conciliatory.

"We came," he said, "to escort you back again. We have a guard of honor here fitting for any bridegroom."

"You are uncommonly kind," replied the Professor, "but the parade is rather unnecessary. I am not going back just at present."

"I promised Bragwaine that you would return with us," said the Prince, sternly.

"Well, you ought not to make rash promises," replied the Professor, with firmness.

"You will go, of course?"

"Of course I will not go."

"Bragwaine is waiting for you."

"That," said the Professor, "is a matter of perfect indifference to me."

"I will not be trifled with, sir," said the Prince, angrily.

"Nor will I," exclaimed the Professor. "Let us understand one another. I do not wish to marry any one. I did not ask your daughter to marry me, and I have never consented to the union. I tell you now that I positively and absolutely refuse to be forced to marry her or any other woman. I will do as I please about it; not as you please."

"Seize him," shrieked the Prince to his attendants.

"Stand off," said the Professor, presenting his revolver. "I'll kill the man who approaches me. I shall put up with this foolishness no longer."

One of the knights rode toward him. The Professor fired, and the cavalier's horse rolled in the dust. The Prince and his people were stupefied with astonishment.

At this juncture, Baron Bors, Sir Dinadan, Sir Agravaine, Sir Bleoberis, and Miss Baffin emerged from the castle. Miss Baffin flew to her father, and flung her arms about him. The Professor kissed her tenderly, and as he did so, his eye caught sight of the wire of the telephone which he had arranged for Ysolt and Sir Bleoberis. A happy thought struck him. Advancing, he said to the Prince:

"It is useless for us to quarrel over this matter. Baron Bors has here an oracle. Let us consult that."

Then the Professor whispered something to Miss Baffin, who withdrew unobserved and went into the castle.

The Prince was at first indisposed to condescend to accept the offer, but his curiosity finally overcame his pride.

"Step this way," said the Professor. "Ask your questions through this," handing him the mouthpiece, "and put this to your ear for the answer."

"What shall I say?" inquired the Prince.

"Ask if it is right that I should marry your daughter."

The Prince put the question, and the answer came.

"What does the oracle say?" asked the Professor.

"It says you shall not," replied the Prince, looking a good deal scared.

"Are you satisfied?" said the Professor.

The Prince did not answer, but he looked as if he suspected a trick of some kind, and would like to impale Professor Baffin with his lance, if he dared.

He was about to turn away in disgust, when Sir

Agravaine, who stood beside him, in a few half-whispered words explained to him the method by which the Professor had imposed upon him.

In a raging fury, the Prince rode up to the Professor, and would have assailed him; but Baron Bors advanced and said:

"This gentleman is unarmed, and unused to our methods of combat. He is my guest, and he has saved my daughter. I will fight his battles."

The Prince threw his glove at the Baron's feet. Baron Bors called for his armor and his horse, and when he was ready he took his place opposite to his antagonist, and waited the signal for the contest.

"This," said the Professor, "is probably the most asinine proceeding upon record. Because I won't marry Sagramor's daughter, Sagramor is going to fight with a man who never saw his daughter."

The combat was not a long one. At the first shock both knights were unhorsed; but, drawing their swords, they rushed together and hacked at each other until the sparks flew in showers from their armor.

The Baron fought well, but presently the Prince's sword struck his shoulder with a blow which carried the blade down through the steel plate, and caused the blood to spurt forth. The Baron fell to the earth; and Prince Sagramor,

AT THE FIRST SHOCK BOTH KNIGHTS WERE UNHORSED. Page 98.

remembering the small number of his attendants, and the probability that he might be assailed by the Baron's people, mounted his horse and slowly trotted away without deigning to look at Professor Baffin. They carried the Baron tenderly into the castle, and put him to bed. The wound was a terrible one, and the Professor perceived that the chances of his recovery, under the rude medical treatment that could be obtained, were not very favorable. After doing what he could to help the sufferer, he withdrew from the room, and left the Baron with Lady Bors and the medical practitioner who was ordinarily employed by the family.

Miss Baffin, with Sir Dinadan, awaited her father in the hall. This was the first opportunity he had had to greet her. After some preliminary conversation, and after the Professor had expressed to Sir Dinadan his regret that the Baron should have been injured, the Professor said:

"And now, Tilly, my love, how have you been employing yourself during my absence?"

Miss Baffin blushed.

"Have you kept the journal regularly?" asked the Professor.

"Not so *very* regularly," replied Miss Baffin.

"I have a number of interesting and extraordinary things for you to record," said the Professor. "Has nothing of a remarkable character happened here during my absence?"

"Oh, yes," said Miss Baffin.

"I have learned to smoke," said Sir Dinadan.

"Indeed," said the Professor with a slight pang. "And how many cigars have you smoked?"

"Only one," replied the Knight. "It made me ill for two days. I think, perhaps, I shall give up smoking."

"I would advise you to. It is a bad habit," said the Professor, "and expensive. And then, you know, cigars are so dreadfully scarce, too."

"The Lady Tilly was very kind to me while I was ill. I believe I was delirious once or twice; and I was so touched by her sweet patience that I again proposed to her."

"While you were delirious?" asked the Professor.

"Oh, no; when I had recovered."

"What did you say to that, Tilly?" asked Professor Baffin.

"I referred him to you," replied Miss Baffin.

"But what will the Baron say?" asked the Professor.

"He and my mother have given their consent," said Sir Dinadan. "They declared that I could not have pleased them better than by making such a choice."

"Well, I don't know," said the Professor, reflectively. "I like you first-rate, and if I felt certain we were going to stay here —"

"I will go with you if you leave the island," said Sir Dinadan, eagerly.

"And then you know, Din," continued the Professor familiarly, "Tilly is highly educated, while you — Well, you know you must learn to read, and write, and cipher, the very first thing."

"I have been giving him lessons while you were away," said Miss Baffin.

"How does he get along?"

"Quite well. He can do short division with a little help, and he has learned as far as the eighth line in the multiplication table."

"Eight eights are sixty-four, eight nines are seventy-two, eight tens are eighty," said Sir Dinadan, triumphantly.

"Well," said the Professor, "if Tilly loves you, and you love Tilly, I shall make no objection."

"Oh, thank you," exclaimed both of the lovers.

"But, I tell you what, Din, you are getting a good bargain. There is no finer girl, or a smarter one either, on the globe. You people here cannot half appreciate her."

For more than a week, Baron Bors failed to show any signs of improvement, and the Professor thought he perceived clearly that his case was fast getting beyond hope. He deemed it prudent, however, to keep his opinion from the members of the Baron's family. But the Baron himself soon reached the same conclusion, and one day Lady

Bors came out of his room to summon Sir Dinadan, Ysolt, Sir Bleoberis, who was now formally betrothed to Ysolt, and the Professor, to the Baron's bedside.

The Baron said to them, in a feeble voice, that he felt his end approaching, and that he desired to give some instructions, and to say farewell to his family. Then he addressed himself first to Sir Dinadan, and next to Ysolt. When he had finished speaking to them he said to Lady Bors,—

"And now, Ettard, a final word to you. I am going away, and you will need another friend, protector, companion, husband. Have you ever thought of any one whom you should like, other than me?"

"Never, never, never," said Lady Bors, sobbing.

"Let me advise you, then. Who would be more likely to fill my place in your heart acceptably than our good and wise and wonderful friend Sir Baffin?"

"Good gracious!" exclaimed the Professor with a start.

"Your son is to marry his daughter; and she will be happy to be here with him in the castle. Promise me that you will try to love him."

"Yes, I will try," said Lady Bors, wiping her eyes and seeming, upon the whole, rather more cheerful.

"That," said the Baron, "does not altogether

satisfy me. I place upon you my command that you shall marry him. Will you consent to obey?"

"I will consent to anything, so that your last hour may be happier," said Lady Bors with an air of resignation. She was supported during the trial, perhaps, by the reflection that in dealing with lumbago Professor Baffin had no superior in the kingdom.

Father Anselm was announced. "Withdraw, now," said the Baron to all of his family but Lady Bors. "I must speak with the Hermit."

Professor Baffin encountered the Hermit at the door. The holy man stopped long enough to say that a huge ship had come near to the shore upon which the Professor had landed, and that it was anchored there. From its mast, Father Anselm said, fluttered a banner of red and white stripes with a starry field of blue.

The Professor's heart beat fast. For a moment he could hardly control his emotion. He resolved to go at once to the shore and to take his daughter with him. Withdrawing her from her companions the two strolled slowly out from the castle into the park. Then, hastening their steps, they passed towards the shore. In a few moments they reached it, and there, sure enough, they saw a barque at anchor, while from her mast-head floated the American flag.

A boat belonging to the barque had come to

the shore to obtain water from the stream. Professor Baffin entered into conversation with the officer who commanded the boat. The vessel proved to be the *Mary L. Simpson*, of Martha's Vineyard, bound from the Azores to New York. When the Professor had explained to the officer that he and his daughter were Americans, the mate invited them to come aboard so that he could introduce them to the captain.

"Shall we go, my child?" asked the Professor.

"If we can return in a very few moments, we might go," said Miss Baffin.

They entered the boat, and when they reached the vessel, they were warmly greeted by Captain Magruder.

While they were talking with him in his cabin the air suddenly darkened, and the captain rushed out upon deck. Almost before he reached it a terrific gale struck the barque, and she began to drag her anchors. Fortunately the wind blew off shore, and the captain, weighing anchor, let the barque drive right out to sea. The Professor was about to remark to Miss Baffin that he feared there was small chance of his ever seeing the island again, when a lurch of the vessel threw him over. His head struck the sharp corner of the captain's chest, and he became unconscious.

When Professor Baffin regained his senses, he found that he was lying in a berth in a ship's cabin. Some one was sitting beside him, —

"Is that you, Tilly?" he asked, in a faint voice.

"Yes, pa; I am glad you are conscious again. Can I give you anything?"

"Have I been long unconscious, Tilly?"

"You have been very ill for several days; delirious sometimes."

"Is the captain going back to the island?"

"Going back to the *what*, pa?"

"To the Island. It must have seemed dreadfully heartless for us to leave the castle while the Baron was dying."

"While the Baron was dying! What do you mean?"

"Why, Baron Bors could not have lived much longer. I am afraid Sir Dinadan will think hard of us."

"I haven't the least idea what you are talking about. Poor pa! your mind is beginning to wander again. Turn over, and try to go to sleep."

Professor Baffin was silent for a moment. Then he said, —

"Tilly, do you mean to say you never heard of Baron Bors?"

"Never."

"And that you were never engaged to Sir Dinadan?"

"Pa, how absurd! Who are these people?"

"Were you not upon the island with me, at the castle?"

"How could we have gone upon an island, pa, when we were taken from the raft by the ship?"

"Tilly, my child, when I get perfectly well I shall have to tell you of the most extraordinary series of circumstances that has come under my observation during the whole course of my existence!"

Then Professor Baffin closed his eyes and fell into a doze, and Miss Baffin went up to tell the surgeon of the ship *Undine*, from Philadelphia to Glasgow, that her father seemed to be getting better.

THE CITY OF BURLESQUE:

An Account of some of the Inhabitants Thereof.

CHAPTER I.

THE COWDRICKS. — A CONJUGAL CHAT. — LEONIE. — A RISING ARTIST. — A PROPOSAL. — SWEETHEARTS.

CCUPYING a very comfortable position in an easy-chair, Mr. Cowdrick, banker, sat in his library before a blazing fire.

The Fate that arranges coincidences, and provides for the fitness of things, could not have persuaded Mr. Cowdrick to choose a more characteristic method of warming himself; for it was a sham fire. Some skilful worker in clay had produced a counterfeit presentment of a heap of logs, with the bark, the bits of moss, the knots, and the drops of sap exuding from the ends, all admirably imitative of nature. But the logs were hollow, and a hidden pipe, upon occasion, filled them with gas, which, as it escaped through imperceptible holes, was ignited, to burn as though it fed upon the inconsumable logs.

The library room was handsomely decorated in accordance with the prevailing modes. Upon the wall were fastened porcelain plates, bearing beautiful designs, but wholly useless for the purpose for which plates were originally devised. Mr. Cowdrick realized that as a mere matter of reason it would be as sensible to put a fireplace in the ceiling, or to cover his library table with the door-mat, as to adorn his wall with a dinner-plate; but, like some of the rest of us Mr. Cowdrick surrendered his private convictions to the suggestions of fashion.

Upon Mr. Cowdrick's shelves and mantels were cups and saucers of curious wares, which were to be looked at and not used; and in his cabinets were jugs and bottles, which existed that they might contribute to the pleasure of the eye rather than to the pleasure of the palate. The bookcases, made with the best art of the workman, after the most approved designs, were filled with richly-bound volumes, into which Mr. Cowdrick had never cared to look since he bought them by the cubic foot; and which, in some instances, considered themes which would not have interested the banker in the slightest degree, even if he had examined them, and had been gifted with the capacity to comprehend them.

Upon the mantel ticked a clock, so fine that it had to be kept under glass, and which had never been known to indicate the time correctly during twenty-four consecutive hours. The chairs and the sofas were made of material so costly that Mrs. Cowdrick had them draped continually in closely-fitting brown-linen covers, so that, in fact, it was somewhat difficult to comprehend why the expensive and delicate fabrics beneath should have been employed at all, seeing that they were perpetually doomed to hide their loveliness.

Mr. Cowdrick sat looking at the deceitful fire in front of him, and as he mused he smoked an excellent cigar. His reverie was presently disturbed by the entrance of Mrs. Cowdrick to the room. Mrs. Cowdrick was a woman in middle life, of rounded figure and pleasing face; and she was clad, at this moment, in rich and tasteful dress. She held in her hand a bit of canvas, upon which she was working, in worsted, a pattern which was intended to convey to the observer the impression that it was of Japanese origin; but really it was as great a sham as Mr. Cowdrick's fire.

Mrs. Cowdrick drew a chair near to that of her husband. Her first act, when she had taken her seat, was to clap her hands vigorously together two or three times, in ineffectual efforts to catch and to crush a fluttering moth-fly.

This is a form of exercise that is very dear to the female heart, but rarely is it productive of any practical results. Calculated in horse-powers, it may fairly be estimated that the amount of force expended annually by the sex upon the work of annihilating moth-flies would be sufficient to raise one pound two hundred thousand feet high, if any one cared to have a pound at such an elevation; while it is probable that the number of moth-flies actually taken upon the wing within the boundaries of civilization, does not in any one year exceed a few hundreds.

When she had concluded her efforts, without at all injuring the insect, Mrs. Cowdrick resumed her worsted attempt to insult Japanese art, and, as she did so, Mr. Cowdrick, turning his head about lazily, as he sent a whiff of smoke into the air, said,—

"Annie, dear, where is Leonie?"

"She is in her room, I think," replied Mrs. Cowdrick, pleasantly. "She will be down in a few moments."

"I wish to have a little talk with you about her, my love," said Mr. Cowdrick. "I have been thinking that it is high time Leonie had found a husband. Let me see; how old is she now?"

"In her twenty-ninth year, really," replied Mrs. Cowdrick; "but then, you know, she does not acknowledge more than twenty-five years to her friends. Leonie is an exceedingly prudent girl."

"But, of course," remarked Mr. Cowdrick, "she cannot keep that up forever. As she grows older she will have to allow a year or two, every now and then; and, after a while, you know, people will begin to count for themselves."

"I have urged that upon her," said Mrs. Cowdrick, "and I think she fully realizes it. Her hair is becoming thinner every week, and there would be no hope of her hiding the truth if the fashion did not permit her easily to cover the bald place upon the top of her head."

"She is no longer the young girl she once was," said Mr. Cowdrick with an air of sadness which seemed to indicate his disappointment at the refusal of Time to make an exception in the case of Leonie.

"No," said Mrs. Cowdrick; "she is beginning to ascertain that she has nerves, and she has to take iron every morning. At the pic-nic in September she tried to appear as girlish as she could; but I noticed, while she was skipping the rope with those little chits of Mrs. Parker's, that she would catch her breath convulsively every time she went up; and you know she was in bed with lumbago for three days afterward."

"She must marry," said Mr. Cowdrick, with emphasis. "The case is getting desperate. I will speak to her about it to-night. I wish her, before I quit home, to have herself engaged to some one who is able to support her handsomely."

"How soon will it be necessary for you to fly?" asked Mrs. Cowdrick.

"Before the end of next week, at the very latest, Matters are fast approaching a crisis at the bank.

We might have pulled through after the failure of Snell and Adam, to whom, as one of the directors was a partner, we lent a large sum upon bogus collateral; and I did not despair even when Pinyard, Moon and Company, with whom I had a silent interest, went under just after obtaining that last hundred thousand of us; but I heard to-day that J. P. Hunn and Co. are very much embarrassed, and as we have hypothecated some good collaterals deposited with us by our best customers in order to keep Hunn on his legs, his failure will inevitably result in the exposure of the whole business."

"And how much, dear, is the bank short?" asked Mrs. Cowdrick, kindly.

"A full million and a quarter at the lowest estimate. We can't tell exactly, because the accounts have been so much falsified to hide the deficiency. But the capital has gone, and with it the bulk of the money belonging to the depositors; and as I say, a whole lot of collateral securities, placed in our hands by some of the best men in town. It's a bad business! They will make it hot for us, I am afraid."

"But then, dear, you will save something from the wreck, you said?"

"Oh, yes! Pinyard told me that he thought he and I would come out with two or three hundred thousand apiece, if we can manage the creditors of his firm so that they will take twenty-five per cent. of their claims in settlement. That, however, is only a possibility."

"If the crash is coming so soon," said Mrs. Cowdrick, with a thoughtful air, "there are some little things I should like to get at once."

"What are they?"

"Why, you know, Henry, I want a sealskin sacque for this winter, and I had thought of buying a pair of plain diamond earrings. Couldn't I get them, say to-morrow, and have them charged, and then let the dealers just come in with the rest of your creditors when you arrange a settlement?"

"Certainly, my love! get them immediately, of course. It is your last chance. I have not yet gotten into such a position that I cannot provide comforts for my family! Tell Leonie to make any little purchases she may need, also. I might as well go to ruin for a large amount as for a small one. A few hundreds more or less will not matter."

As Mr. Cowdrick spoke, Leonie entered the room. She was elegantly and fashionably dressed, and her face was wreathed with smiles. She ran up to her father as a child might have done, and with a girlish laugh kissed him; then, drawing a footstool close to him, she sat down beside him and placed her arm upon his knee. Mr. Cowdrick stroked her head affectionately, with a tenderness that was partly induced by fondness and partly by a recollection of what Mrs. Cowdrick had said of Leonie's method of disguising the bare place upon her crown.

After reflecting for a moment in silence, Mr. Cowdrick said, —

"I want to ask my little girl if she has lost her heart to any one yet?"

Leonie blushed, and straightening herself up she said nervously, but with traces of a smile about her lips, —

"Lost my heart, papa! What do you mean?"

"I mean, my dear child, that it is high time you had obtained a husband and settled yourself for life. It is important you should marry as speedily as possible."

"Oh, papa!" said Leonie, hiding her face in her hands.

"To speak plainly, darling," said Mr. Cowdrick, "your poor father's affairs are in such a condition that a judicious matrimonial alliance is almost necessary to your future happiness. You understand me, of course; I am not at all sure of my financial future."

"I am very sorry," said Leonie.

"Of course you are," replied Mr. Cowdrick, "but being sorry is not enough. I should bear the calamity, when it comes, much more bravely if I were assured that my dear child had a good and affluent husband to console her amid the troubles that will befall her family. Is there no one to whom you could give your affection if you tried? If you tried right hard, just to please your poor old papa?"

Leonie hesitated before answering, and then she said, —

"Yes, papa, there is!"

"I am glad to hear that! Who is it, darling?"

"You will not be angry with me, papa, if I tell you, will you? I *have* given my love to some one, and that some one is — is — Mr. Weems, the artist!"

"What!" exclaimed Mr. Cowdrick, in a voice that indicated mingled surprise and indignation. "Not Julius Weems, the painter?"

"You don't mean to say you are actually engaged to be married to that young man?" said Mrs. Cowdrick, vehemently.

"Yes, I am engaged to him," said Leonie, putting her forehead down upon the arm of her father's chair. "He proposed to me on Tuesday, while you were at the opera."

"And you love him?" asked Mr. Cowdrick.

"Oh, yes," replied Leonie, "I love him; of course I love him, or I never would have accepted him. But I don't mean to say, positively and finally, that I would refuse a better chance if it presented itself. Julius is the only person who seems likely to want me, and certainly he is a great deal better than nobody."

"Yes; but, my dear child," observed Mr. Cowdrick, "a mere husband is nothing. The circumstances of the husband are everything."

"And Mr. Weems is poor as poverty," added Mrs. Cowdrick.

"Oh, no, mamma, you are mistaken," said Leonie. "Julius is in very comfortable circumstances. He has a very profitable business."

"He has, has he?" said Mr. Cowdrick. "Well, I can't imagine where it can be. I never have seen any of his pictures."

"Why, papa," rejoined Leonie with a slight laugh. "Julius says that you have two of his best works in your gallery."

"I have," exclaimed Mr. Cowdrick, in astonishment. "I think not."

"He says so, at any rate."

"Which are they?"

"Why, the 'Leader and the Swan,' by Correggio, and the 'St. Lawrence,' by Titian."

"Leonie, that is ridiculous," said Mr. Cowdrick, warmly.

"Perfectly absurd," remarked Mrs. Cowdrick.

"But Julius declares he really did paint them. He says he paints nothing but 'old masters'; that they bring the best prices, and that there is always an active demand for them. He wants me to come to his studio to see a splendid Murillo he has just finished. He is making money rapidly."

"In that case, Leonie," said Mr. Cowdrick, with a slight touch of bitterness, as he thought of the prices he had paid for his Correggio and his Titian, but with a certain cheerfulness, gained from his suddenly formed resolution to realize on them to-morrow — "in that case, we must regard Mr. Weems differently. He appears at least to be an enterprising young man, and possibly he may do well."

"You had better arrange to see him at once, dear," said Mrs. Cowdrick, "so that you can ascertain what his income is, and how soon the wedding can be arranged."

"I will do so," replied Mr. Cowdrick. "But my child, did you tell him anything? Does he know that you have already been engaged three times? Does he know that you were affianced to old Mr. Baxter, who gained your affection under the pretence that he was a millionaire, only to tread upon the holiest of your emotions with the scandalous revelation that he was living upon a paltry pension?"

"No, papa, I did not think it worth while to disturb Julius with such matters as that. What does he care for my past? No more than I care for his!"

"Do you think he suspects your age, dear?" asked Mrs. Cowdrick.

"I am certain he does not. You know I falsified the date in the family Bible, and last evening I got him to look over it with me, under pretense of searching for a text. When I showed him the record, laughingly, he pretended to be surprised. He said he should never have supposed me to be a day over twenty-three."

Mr. Cowdrick slowly winked that one of his eyes which was upon the side towards his wife, and then he said, —

"Well, Leonie, we will see about it. There are some things about the match to recommend it, although I cannot say Weems is precisely the man I should have chosen for you. However, you are the person who is most deeply interested, and I suppose we must let you choose for yourself. I wish you would ask Mr. Weems to call to see me to-morrow evening concerning the matter."

"He will be here to-night, papa," replied Leonie. "He said he would call to make a formal proposal for my hand."

"Very well; that will do nicely. The sooner we reach a distinct understanding, the better."

Before many moments had elapsed, Mr. Julius Weems was announced by the servant, whereupon Mrs. Cowdrick and Leonie withdrew. When Mr. Weems entered the room, Mr. Cowdrick greeted him politely, but with dignified gravity. Mr. Weems was somewhat nervous. Mr. Cowdrick clearly perceived that he had reduced himself to a condition of misery with a resolution to obtain, if possible during this visit, the paternal blessing upon his proposed alliance with Leonie.

The current theory is that the most difficult of the processes by which the state of marriage is approached, is the first declaration of affection to the object of it ; and it may be possible that most men, upon reviewing their conduct upon such occasions, are inclined to believe that they made fools of themselves. But, as a matter of fact, it is nearly certain that those who make a careful survey of their experiences will be likely to admit that the most trying ordeal through which the lover is compelled to go is that of ascertaining what opinion of the matter is held by the father of his sweetheart. If there is a reasonable certainty that the loved one will accept him, he is at least sure of the most acute and delicious sympathy when he summons up courage enough to take her little hand in his and to give voice to his feelings ; and the difference of sex enables the performance to assume the most romantic aspect. But to face a cold, practical man of the world with a lot of sentiment, and to plunge boldly into an explanation to him of a fervid passion which he regards in the prosiest fashion possible, requires bravery of a very high order. And the man who can approach such a task with perfect self-possession, and positive command of his mental faculties and of his utterance, has a nervous system that ordinary men may envy.

For a moment after Mr. Weems seated himself upon the other side of the fire-place from Mr. Cowdrick, there was an embarrassing silence. Then Mr. Cowdrick, to open the way for his visitor, remarked that it had been a very disagreeable day.

"Very," said Mr. Weems. "Uncommonly damp and chilly, even for this time of year."

"Yesterday was far from pleasant also," observed Mr. Cowdrick.

"Wasn't it abominable?" replied Mr. Weems. "There will be a great deal of sickness if this kind of weather continues."

"The prospect," rejoined Mr. Cowdrick, "is that it will. There are no signs of a clear day to-morrow."

"I'm afraid not," returned Mr. Weems.

Then Mr. Cowdrick looked into the fire, and relapsed into silence. The weather of the past, the present, and the future having been considered, there really seemed to be nothing more to be said upon that particular topic. It would be curious to ascertain what men, who are in a stress for something to talk about, fall back upon in those regions where there is steadfast sunshine during half of every year, and unremitting rain during the other half.

"How is Miss Leonie?" said Mr. Weems, suddenly, and with an air of desperation.

"Quite well, thank you," answered Mr. Cowdrick.

"Well, Mr. Cowdrick, I called this evening to speak to you about her," continued Weems, with a determination to make the plunge and have it over.

"Indeed!"

"Yes, sir. In fact, Mr. Cowdrick, your daughter has consented to become my wife, and I wish to obtain, if I may, your approval of the match. May I have it?"

"Really, Mr. Weems, this is so unexpected. I was so little prepared for such an announcement that I hardly know what——. My answer would depend somewhat upon circumstances, I may say, I have no objection to you personally; but I know nothing of your prospects in your profession."

"They are first-rate. I sold a picture to-day for five thousand dollars; and that is by no means an infrequent occurrence."

"Who bought it?"

"St. Cadmus's church. It is an altar piece; very handsome and old; by Michael Angelo. You see, I give you my secret; in confidence, of course."

"Yes," said Mr. Cowdrick, "I am a regular attendant at St. Cadmus's and I was one of four subscribers for that picture. The balance of the amount we made up by mortgaging the organ. Mr. Tunicle, the incumbent, said it was indisputably genuine."

"Oh, well," said Mr. Weems, laughing; "if it looks like a genuine one, and everybody thinks it is genuine, what difference is there? The people are every bit as happy as if it were real. If one of my pictures sells better with the name of some old chap who has been dead for two or three centuries tagged to it, why shouldn't I let it go in that way? It does not hurt him, and it helps me."

"From your point of view the theory is excellent; but from mine, as the owner of a couple of old masters, it looks a little thin."

"Well, to be fair," said Mr. Weems, "I acknowledge that I painted those you have, but I am willing to find you a market for them, to oblige you; or I will sell you two or three more, if you prefer it. I have just run off a fine Salvator Rosa, and a Titian, as kind of 'pot-boilers,' and you can have them for almost nothing if you want them."

"Thank you, no," said Mr. Cowdrick. "My interest in art is gradually cooling off. And then, besides, if you are going to turn out pictures every time you want a suit of clothes, or a box of cigars, it seems likely there will soon be a glut of old masters in the market."

"But to come back to the point, Mr. Cowdrick," said Mr. Weems. "What may I accept as your decision respecting my claim to your daughter's hand?"

"Have you ever had an affair of this kind before, Mr. Weems? Pardon me for asking. Is Leonie your first love?"

"Well, you know, every man does foolish things in his youth. I have been involved in one or two trifling matters of the sort. But I am a careful man, and to avoid any unpleasant demonstrations in the future, I have procured formal decrees of divorce from eleven different girls; all, in fact, with whom I have ever had any acquaintance that was at all sentimental. I obtained six decrees from the State of Indiana, at a cost of ten dollars apiece, and the remainder from Utah, at a little higher rate."

"And you were never married to any of the parties?"

"Oh, no! merely knew them; took them out driving, or danced with them at balls. Some of them are married to other men. But, you know, a man is never certain what may happen; women are so queer; and so I concluded to destroy all the chances of anything turning up, and I have the legal documents to show for it. Leonie's happiness is perfectly safe with me, I assure you."

"Your course seems to me a prudent one, at any rate," remarked Mr. Cowdrick; "but then, of course, it is possible for a man to be a little too far-sighted for the comfort of other people. How do I know, for instance, that you haven't taken the precaution to file away among your papers a divorce from Leonie?"

"Oh, well," said Mr. Weems, laughing, "you

know I wouldn't go quite that far. I admit that I have half a dozen blank decrees, which I can fill up to meet emergencies, but I pledge you my word of honor that I will never put her name in one. I love her too dearly."

"Do you believe you would love her if she were poor; or if she were to become poor?"

"Yes, certainly; of course," answered Mr. Weems. And then he added mentally, "I wonder if anything is the matter? I'll inquire about the old man's financial standing the first thing in the morning."

"Well," said Mr. Cowdrick, "I hardly know. Leonie is very dear to me. I have not contemplated an early marriage for her. It would be a terrible wrench upon my heartstrings. What would you do if I refused my consent?"

"Try to submit with what patience I could command, I suppose. But you will not refuse, will you?"

Mr. Cowdrick did not respond at once. He had rather cherished the hope that Weems would elope with Leonie, and save him the expense of a wedding outfit and of a wedding festival, besides relieving him of all responsibility. But he saw now that it would not be safe to take the chances.

"Well, Mr. Weems," he said, at length, " so far as I am concerned, I think I may say that if Leonie wishes to marry you, she can. But we must ask her mother about it. It will be a terrible shock to poor Mrs. Cowdrick. I will call her in."

When Mrs. Cowdrick entered the room with Leonie, Mr. Cowdrick said, —

"My dear, Mr. Weems, here, has formally proposed for the hand of Leonie, and I have given my consent, provided you also would do so."

Mrs. Cowdrick replied by a shriek, after which she flung herself into a chair, and, with an expensive handkerchief to her face, she sobbed hysterically.

"Ma is doing that to show how well she can pose," said Leonie, in a whisper to Weems. "She used to be splendid in private theatricals."

Mrs. Cowdrick sprang up, and in tones of apparently intense excitement she said, — "No, no! I cannot let her go! It is impossible! It is so unexpected, so sudden! My child, my poor, darling child! To be torn ruthlessly from the arms of her dear mother! I cannot bear it! It will kill me!" and Mrs. Cowdrick flung her arms wildly about Leonie and wept.

Leonie seemed quite calm. She lowered her shoulder slightly, to incline her mother's head, so that her tears would fall upon the floor instead of upon her dress.

Mr. Cowdrick comforted her, reasoned with her, and showed her that, after all, Leonie's happiness was at stake. To promote her happiness, her parents must be willing to make some sacrifices, and she must try to brace herself to meet the trial, hard as it was. Mrs. Cowdrick's agitation gradually decreased, as her husband spoke; and when she had rested upon the sofa for a moment, and helped her nerves by inhaling salts from a gilded smelling-bottle, she said:

"If it must be, it must! Take her, Julius! Take her, and love her, and cherish her, so that she will never rue having been torn from the parental nest!"

"I promise you faithfully to do my best," replied Mr. Weems.

"And now, my children," said Mr. Cowdrick, as his voice trembled with emotion, "I give you an old man's blessing! May you be happy in each other's love until life shall end!"

Then Mr. Cowdrick wiped his eyes, and taking Mrs. Cowdrick on his arm, they went upstairs to discuss some method by which the marriage could be celebrated before the crash came at the bank.

"And you are mine at last, darling!" said Mr. Weems, as he pushed his chair up close to Leonie's and took her hand in his.

In reply she nestled her head up against his shoulder, and her thoughts went out dreamily over the past. Old Mr. Baxter and her two other lovers had made precisely the same remark to her under similar circumstances, and she had responded to them in the same manner. Life is an endless round of repetitions.

"Sweet face!" said Mr, Weems, patting it tenderly, as if he were a trifle uncertain of the permanent nature of the color. "Did you know, darling, that I put your face in one of my recent pictures?"

"Oh, Julius! Did you?"

"Yes, dear, I gave it to my full length of St. Ethelberta, by Rubens."

"Is it a good likeness?"

"I think it is. But," said Mr. Weems thoughtfully, "it didn't sell! That is, I mean, no person of really good taste has inspected it yet."

"And you painted it because you loved me, did you?"

"Oh, yes! Certainly! Of course!"

"How fortunate it was that I could return your love, wasn't it? Julius, what would you have done if I had refused you?"

"Done? Why, it would have mortified me dreadfully. I don't believe I should have had any appetite for a week or more."

"Some disappointed lovers," said Leonie almost reproachfully, and with an air of chagrin, "become utterly desperate and try to take their own lives."

"Oh, I know," replied Mr. Weems. "Dreadful, isn't it? But I generally try to bear up under misery. It's a duty."

"Could you bear misery for my sake, Julius? Do you think your love would endure if poverty should overtake us? Bitter, blinding poverty?"

"I am sure I could," replied Mr. Weems with a renewed determination to discover in the morning if Mr. Cowdrick's credit had been impaired.

"You believe, then, that love in a cottage is a possibility, do you, dear?" asked Leonie.

"Yes, darling; possible, but not fascinating. My observation is that love, upon the whole, has a better chance in a commodious mansion with all of the modern conveniences; with gas, water and a boy to answer the front-door bell. Love, darling, is like some other things in this world — it thrives better when it is comfortable."

"Have you thought about our wedding, dear?" asked Leonie. "Where will we go upon our wedding journey? Wouldn't it be splendid to take a trip to Europe?"

The suggestion did not seem to excite any great amount of enthusiasm in the heart of Mr. Weems. He said: "It would be very nice, but I am afraid it would be almost too expensive, unless your pa — Did your pa say anything about it?" asked Julius, with a faint expectation that Mr. Cowdrick may have intended to include a handsome cheque among the presents.

"No," replied Leonie; "he said nothing, Only I thought may-be you might want to go."

"So I do, my love, but business is a trifle dull just now. I am afraid we shall have to wait until the prevailing prejudice against Rubens and St. Ethelberta blows over, as it were. I thought perhaps we might make a short trip to Boston and back. How would that suit you?"

"I would be satisfied with it, dear, of course," said Leonie.

Mr. Weems heard her answer with the serene consciousness that he had a free pass for two over that particular route, and that even upon a wedding journey there would be no need to be actually riotous in the matter of hotel expenses.

"And when we get home, and settle down, may I keep a parrot, Julius?"

"Well," replied Mr. Weems, "the question is sudden and somewhat irrelevant, but I should think you might; provided, of course, you selected one that has not been taught to use profane language, and to imitate a screeching wheelbarrow with too great accuracy."

"You are so kind! And, Julius?"

"What, sweet?"

"If papa should die, could dear mamma come to live with us?"

"I'll tell you what, Leonie, suppose we postpone the consideration of some of these distressing contingencies until they actually present themselves! I am perfectly willing to wrestle with a grief when it comes, but there is no use of putting crape on a door-knocker until there is bereavement in the family circle."

"That is true, dear. And, Julius?"

"Well, my love?"

"Whenever you can't come to see me, will you write to me? I want you to send me, at least once every day, a dear, kind, affectionate letter, full of love; won't you, dear?"

"I will, if you will promise faithfully to burn them," replied Julius, as his prudent mind grasped the possibility of some unfortunate future misunderstanding, in which ardent love-letters might have a damagin geffect upon the case of the defendant. "That is, pretty nearly every day."

"Thus far," continued Leonie, "I have kept all that you have written. I have read them over, and over, and over, and kissed them again and again. The sweet verses you have sent to me I have learned by heart."

"Have you, darling?" said Mr. Weems, with a feeling of pride in his success as a poet.

"Shall I repeat them to you?"

"If you will, dearest," replied Mr. Weems, with the air of a man who was conscious that he had turned off rather a good thing in the way of verses.

"Let me see," said Leonie, leaning back in her chair, "how do they begin? Oh, yes!"

'Sweetheart, if I could surely choose
    The aptest word in passion's speech,
And all its subtlest meaning use
    With eloquence, your soul to teach,
Still, forced by its intensity,
Sweetheart, my love would voiceless be.

'Sweetheart, though all the days and hours
    Sped by, with love in sharpest stress,
To find some reach of human powers
    Its faintest impulse to express;
Till Time merged in Eternity,
Sweetheart, my love would voiceless be.'

Are they not beautiful?" asked Leonie, as she concluded.

"Very beautiful," responded Mr. Weems, with a faint impression that it might perhaps pay him to abandon the old masters, and to grasp the resounding lyre, with a resolution to thrum it during the remainder of his life.

"'Sweetheart' is a name I always liked," said Leonie. "You called me your 'rosebud,' in your last letter; but somehow it did not please me so much as 'sweetheart;' it was not so natural."

"Twenty-five years *is* old for a rosebud," said Mr. Weems, absently.

"Yes," replied Leonie; "and does it not seem odd, Julius, that we who have been apart so long should now be united forever, and that we should go down the current of time together until the end?"

While she was speaking, the elegant clock, from beneath its crystal covering, chimed out the hour of *four*, and the artist, consulting his watch, discovered that the correct time was precisely ten minutes past eleven. He arose from his seat, and fondly embracing Leonie, he kissed her, and bade her good night. She went to the window, and as, by the light of the street lamp, she saw him descending the steps in front of the house, she waved her hand toward him. Then turning, she proceeded to the hall, and up the stairs to bed, murmuring to herself, —

"Burn them! That *would* be insane!"

CHAPTER II.

SAINT CADMUS'S. — CHURCH MATTERS OF IMPORTANCE. — FATHER KRUM AND FATHER TUNICLE. — A RIOTOUS SERVICE.

MR. COWDRICK, although making no profession of a special fondness for a religious life, was one of the pillars of St. Cadmus's Church. He had been elected to a place in the vestry; he held two pews; he contributed upon occasion to the Church fund; and Rev. Mr. Tunicle, who was "an advanced Ritualist," found in Mr. Cowdrick an ardent supporter whenever he undertook to introduce innovations in his method of conducting the services.

It did not seem important to Mr. Cowdrick that Mr. Tunicle should always try to produce from the records of the early Church his authority for any new and surprising practice that he wished to adopt. If the thing seemed to Mr. Cowdrick good in itself, if it pleased his eye, and gratified what he chose to consider the æsthetic demands of his nature, he deemed it unnecessary to ask any more questions. He would as soon have thought of inquiring, before he bought a new chair for his library, or a new set of plate for his table, whether his grandfather had established any precedent in the matter of the purchase of chairs and dishes, as to have sought in eccleslological history warrant for the embellishment of the services at St. Cadmus's. It was enough that the worshipers who had the most money, and who were able to pay for novelties, wanted them.

Mr. Tunicle, or Father Tunicle, as his most enthusiastic admirers called him, was a frequent visitor at the house of Mr. Cowdrick. Not only did he find there a great deal of sympathy with his plans, but he liked the society of Leonie, and he was exceedingly anxious to enlist her among the active workers in the church.

He called upon Leonie one evening, shortly after her betrothal to Mr. Weems; and as the artist happened to be out of town, Father Tunicle had an opportunity to enjoy some uninterrupted conversation with the young lady.

"I noticed last Sunday, Father Tunicle," said Leonie, after some preliminary conversation, "that you did not use the velvet sermon-cover I worked for you. I hope you are pleased with it?"

"Oh yes, delighted with it. But then, you know, I couldn't use it last Sunday. The color for the Third Sunday after Epiphany is green, and the sermon cover you know, is violet. I can use it on Septuagesima Sunday, of course. We cannot be too particular about these things in a world that is lying in wickedness."

"Oh, excuse me," said Leonie. "I had gotten the idea, somehow, that violet was the morning color for last Sunday, and red the evening color."

"You are thinking of Quinquagesima Sunday, Miss Cowdrick," said Father Tunicle, smiling gravely. "The color changes upon that day. You must study more carefully the little almanac I gave you. When the Church provides us with good books which may guide us to lives of earnest devotion, it is our duty to read them attentively."

"I will promise to do better in the future," said Leonie, meekly.

"I ought to tell you also," continued Father Tunicle, "that I could not use the Lavabo you worked for me, at all."

"Indeed! Why?"

"Why, instead of making it of plain linen, you made it of damask, and you embroidered it with silk; whereas everything but French red marking cotton or white marking cotton is expressly prohibited by the rules. Nothing in the almanac is stated in plainer terms than this. St. Paul, you know, insisted that things should be done decently and in order, and we are bound to heed his injunction."

"Ah, Father Tunicle, I am afraid I neglect St. Paul as much as I do my almanac. Will you believe I really didn't know that he says anything about plain linen and French red marking cotton? I plead guilty."

"No, Miss Cowdrick, you misunderstand me. I did not mean to indicate that the apostle is the authority for these things. Unhappily he does not allude to them. Whether he ought to have done so, is another question. Our authority for them is more recent, but it is not to be despised upon that account."

"Of course not."

"I have great difficulty in impressing the importance of these things upon the minds of some of our people. Despite my repeated injunctions, Mrs. Battersby brought back from the laundry the altar-cloth filled with starch, and in the midst of my distress over the discovery of this sacrilege, I perceived that the sexton had omitted to pin the fringe to the super-frontal. If we are to be made perfect through suffering, I feel that I am not far from perfection, unless these distressing occurrences shall cease."

"It is terrible," said Leonie, with tender sympathy in her voice.

"By the way, Miss Cowdrick," said the pastor, "to turn to pleasanter themes. Cannot I enlist your more active interest in our church work?

Will you not come into the Sunday-school as a teacher?"

"I am not competent to teach, I fear."

"We can give you a class of girls or a class of boys, as you prefer. The boys' class, which is named, 'Little Lambs of the Flock,' is, I fear, somewhat too unruly for you. Miss Bunner gave it up because the scholars would persist in pinching each other and quarrelling during the lesson. They are so rough and boisterous that I think it will be better to get a male teacher to manage them. But you could take the girls' class, 'The Zealous Workers,' and perhaps persuade the pupils to surrender their present indifference to everything that is being done in either the Sunday-school or the church."

"I will consider the matter, and let you have my answer as speedily as possible," replied Leonie.

"Do, please. And I must speak to your father again about my assistant, Father Krum. He is not in sympathy with me, and it would be better for both of us if he could be removed."

"It is so unfortunate," said Leonie.

"I have told him repeatedly that his stole must always match the color of the frontal of the altar; but you perhaps noticed last Sunday that he came in with a black stole, and, of course, with a green frontal, all hope of a harmonious combination of colors was gone. It spoiled the entire service for me."

"For me too," said Leonie.

"Sometimes I think Krum is wilfully perverse and obstinate. Upon several recent occasions he has read the Epistle upon the Gospel side, and the Gospel upon the Epistle side, and when I remonstrated with him, after church, he was positively offensive. He said that if the people only listened to the Scripture and heeded it, he couldn't see why it made any difference whether he stood upon one side or the other, or balanced himself on top of the chancel rail. Scandalous, wasn't it?"

"Perfectly scandalous."

"He seems to take pleasure in destroying the effect of the finest groupings that I arrange in the chancel with him and the acolytes; and when I proposed to introduce an orchestra, led by Professor Batterini, whom I should dress in a surplice, Krum had the insolence to say that he did not believe that there was any use of trying to preach the Gospel to the poor with a brass band. The man seems to be lost to all sense of reverence."

"Entirely lost," said Leonie.

"And as for praying to the east, that he appears determined not to do. Of course, with the incorrect orientation of the church, we have only a 'supposititious east,' and Krum insists that if I have a right to suppose the north-northwest, I think it is, to be the east, he is equally entitled to suppose the southwest or due south to be east, and so he does as he pleases. When he said, the other day, that in his opinion more depended upon the frame of mind in which the prayers were said, than upon the particular point of the compass towards which the supplications were presented, I did not answer him. Such a man is almost beyond the reach of argument."

Mr. Cowdrick came in while Father Tunicle was speaking; and when the good pastor had rehearsed his grievances to the banker, Mr. Cowdrick said,—

"Father Krum's conduct is subversive of good order and of authority; and if he is allowed to continue he will demoralize the entire congregation. He ought to remember what the Bible says about submitting reverently to one's pastors and spiritual masters. You are his pastor and spiritual master. Isaiah, isn't it, who says that?"

"The quotation, though somewhat inexact," replied Father Tunicle, "is from the Catechism."

"Well, anyhow, he ought to do as you want him to do. That is what we pay him for. And if he refuses to do it, he ought to be dismissed."

"That," said Father Tunicle, "will be difficult to do while he has at least half of the vestrymen with him. I am sorry to say that his obstinacy is countenanced and approved by a number of the lay officers of the church."

"Then we must use force!" exclaimed Mr. Cowdrick. "If we men who put down our money to keep the church in operation cannot be allowed to do as we please, we had better stop contributing. The people who pay for spreading the glad tidings of the Gospel ought to be allowed to spread them in their own way."

"Matters," said Father Tunicle, "are fast approaching a point where something will have to be done. Three times I have instructed Krum to extend only three of his fingers when he pronounces absolution, but he continues to hold out his entire hand, with all his fingers wide open. The last time he did it I noticed that Mrs. Lindsay, who is one of our party, got up and left the church in a rage."

"I saw her go out," said Leonie. "That was the first Sunday upon which she wore her purple velvet bonnet. Everybody was looking at her."

"If he does it again," said Mr. Cowdrick, "I am in favor of shutting the church doors against him and his friends. Peremptory action of some kind becomes a necessity in cases like this."

After some further conversation relative to ecclesiastical and secular matters, Father Tunicle took his leave, and went home, probing the deep recesses of his mind, as he walked along, to find some plan by which he might successfully overcome the resistance offered by the perverse Father Krum to the evangelization of a fallen race.

The next Sunday morning was bright and beautiful. The air was cold, but the sun shone from a clear sky to tempt from their homes the worshipers who, however willing to brave, on week-days, terrific storms sent to keep them from shopping excursions and parties, have not nerve enough upon Sundays to face a cloud no larger than a man's hand.

Those persons who, upon devotional errands intent, walked along the footway near St. Cadmus's church at the hour of morning prayer, perceived that something of an unusual and exciting nature was in progress in and about that purely Gothic edifice. The many whose curiosity succeeded in overcoming their desire to be punctual in their attendance at the sanctuary, paused to observe the proceedings.

A crisis had been reached in the quarrel between Father Tunicle and Father Krum. As the latter, in response to still another request that he would extend but three fingers in his pronunciation of the absolution, had positively, and indeed with vehemence, refused to extend less than four, and had gone so far as to indicate that, under serious provocation, he might even thrust out eight fingers and two thumbs, Father Tunicle's party had resolved that the time had come for them to act.

"It is a terrible thing to do," said Father Tunicle; "but the blood of the martyrs is the seed of the Church; and we must stand up boldly for truth and right, though we die for it."

And so, upon that lovely Sunday morning, when dumb Nature herself seemed to be trying to express, with the glory of her sunshine, and with the pure beauty of her azure sky, her sense of the goodness of her Creator, Father Tunicle and six of his vestrymen, reinforced by a few earnest sympathizers, who were subsequently admitted through a side door by a faithful sexton, took possession of the church.

When Father Krum arrived, the faithful sexton, keeping watch and ward at the aforesaid door, refused to let him in; and when the indignant clergyman demanded a reason for his exclusion, the functionary informed him that his reckless conduct in using four fingers and a thumb, instead of the inferior number warranted by a strict regard for the usages of the primitive Church, had persuaded Father Tunicle and his partisans that, as a shepherd of the sheep, he was a lamentable and dismal, not to say dangerous, failure.

Then Father Krum, in a frame of mind that contained no suggestion of Christian resignation, walked rapidly around to the front of the church, where he found a group of persons, members of the congregation, who were standing before a close-barred door, behind which, in the vestibule, stood Father Tunicle and his adherents. While Father Krum, in the mildest tones that he could command, and with a proper desire not to produce any excitement, explained the situation to the crowd, the six vestrymen who inclined to favor his views, in opposition to those of Father Tunicle, came up, one after the other.

They were taken completely by surprise, and felt they were at a disadvantage. But after some preliminary discussion, they called Mr. Krum aside, and began to consider with him what should be done. Mr. Krum counselled a retreat. His voice was for peace. He urged that a resort to violence at any time, but especially at such a time, would be shocking. But the vestrymen did not agree with him. Mr. Yetts declared that they had a right to enter the church, and that for officers of the church with authority co-equal with theirs to deny that right, was simply monstrous, and not to be endured. Mr. Palfrey, Mr. Green, and the other vestrymen, expressed their full agreement with this proposition.

"But let us try peaceful means, at any rate," said Mr. Krum. "I will knock at the door."

He advanced and knocked. "Who is it?" said a voice from within.

"It is Mr. Krum, six of the vestrymen, and a large portion of the congregation. We wish to enter."

"Can't do it," replied the voice, which was that of the sexton, who had advanced to the front, and had been thrown out upon the picket line in the vestibule.

"Where is Father Tunicle?" asked Mr. Krum.

"He has just begun the service, and has gotten as far as 'dearly beloved brethren.' My orders are that you can't get in until he says the apostolic benediction!"

"Ask one of the vestrymen to come to the window for a moment, please," said Mr. Krum.

Presently one of the front windows was raised to the height of two or three inches, and Mr. Cowdrick peered through the wire netting that protected it.

"What do you want?" asked Mr. Cowdrick.

"We wish to know," said Mr. Yetts, "why we are excluded from this church, and by whose authority?"

"You are excluded," said Mr. Cowdrick, "because we who pay the expenses are determined to run the church in our own way. The door is shut by our authority; by mine!"

"Do you mean to say," asked Mr. Krum, with much mildness, "that you intend to try to make this exclusion permanent?"

"Of course. We have possession and we intend to keep it. Hurry up if you have anything to say; I want to go in and help swell the responses."

"See here, Cowdrick," said Mr. Yetts, fiercely, "if you don't open that door, we will break it down. We're not going to stand any more of this nonsense."

"You'd better not try it," replied Mr. Cowdrick. "I shall summon the police to protect us if you do."

In response to this, Mr. Yetts advanced to the door and kicked it three or four times, viciously. The crowd, which had swollen until it covered the pavement and filled the street, laughed at this demonstration. Mr. Cowdrick, behind the window netting, laughed also. Mr. Yetts, with crimson face, retired in tolerably good order to consult with his friends. Father Krum advised him to give it up.

"Give it up!" exclaimed Mr. Yetts. "I'll show you how I'll give it up!"

Then he and Mr. Green went around the corner for a little space, and returned presently with a somewhat ponderous wooden beam. The four other vestrymen manned it, and aimed it at the door. Bang! went the end against the portal, which bravely withstood the shock. The crowd cheered, and a dozen boys, who regarded the performance with delighted interest, crowded up behind the assaulting column, and betrayed a desire to give additional impetus to Mr. Yetts' battering ram.

The Krum section of the vestry made another charge, striking the door with terrible force, but still failing to effect a breach. At this moment one of Father Tunicle's acolytes emerged from the side-door and attempted to glide down the street in search of a policeman. He was captured by one of the besieging force, and held as a prisoner. He brought the news that Father Tunicle had stopped short in the service when the first blow was struck against the door, and that the entire garrison was now rallied in the vestibule, where they were fortifying the portal with the baptismal font, the episcopal chair, some Sunday-school benches, and a lectern.

Mr. Krum remonstrated with Mr. Yetts, and entreated him not to proceed any further. He urged that it was a dreadful thing for Christian men to create such a disturbance upon the Sabbath-day.

"I don't know about that!" replied Mr. Yetts, who was now warm with wrath and with excitement. "When Peter did wrong didn't Paul 'withstand him to the face'?"

"Yes; but, my dear Mr. Yetts, think of it! St. Paul did not try to batter down the church door on a Sunday morning with a log of wood! You are going too far!"

"Times have changed since then," said Mr. Yetts. "Paul probably never encountered precisely such an emergency. Once more!" exclaimed Mr. Yetts to the assailants. "Give it to 'em hard this time!"

Seizing the beam, the vestrymen and their friends advanced once more to the attack. Three times was the door smitten without effect, but

A RIOTOUS SERVICE. Page 147.

when the fourth blow was struck it gave way, and was flung wide open, revealing Father Tunicle and his friends, standing amid a mass of overturned and wrecked furniture, pale with rage and dismay, and ready to defend with force the citadel which thus was exposed to the enemy.

The crowd sent up a shout of satisfaction, and the intrepid Yetts, with his five vestrymen, regarded their triumph with exultation

What they would have done next, if they had been permitted to press forward through the breach, can only be imagined. For a moment it looked as if beneath that spire which idly pointed these men toward a better country, whence rage and hatred and all evil passions are shut out, and beneath the bell, whose function was to send vibrating through the tremulous air its summons to the temple of the Prince of Peace, there might be a hand-to-hand encounter, in which priest and people should assail each other with furious violence.

But, most happily, at this critical moment, a squad of policemen came upon the scene, and entering the doorway, separated the combatants and prevented any further demonstration.

"Never mind!" exclaimed Mr. Yetts, shaking his fist at the Father Tunicle faction. "We will go to law about it. We shall see who has a right to use this church!"

"As you please!" replied Mr. Sloper, one of the

vestrymen who adhered to Father Tunicle. "We will fight you to the last gasp!"

And then both parties dispersed, leaving the church in charge of the policemen, who closed the door, and took the key to the nearest magistrate.

Taken altogether, the day's proceedings, regarded as the performance of Christian gentlemen, citizens of a Christian country, upon the day designated by Christianity as a day of peace and rest — as a day of devotion to celestial and holy things, could hardly be regarded as encouraging to those hopeful persons who cherish the theory that the world is to be made better by illustrations of the excellence of the advantages of pure religion.

CHAPTER III.

MYSTERIOUS DISAPPEARANCE OF MR. COWDRICK. — THE " CRAB." — " HEAR BOTH SIDES." — A SKELETON DISCOVERED. — A POWERFUL SERMON.

BEFORE another Sunday came, the community was shocked and startled by the announcement that Mr. Cowdrick, the banker, had suddenly and mysteriously disappeared. What had become of him nobody seemed to know. Even Mrs. Cowdrick apparently did not know. The friends who promptly called upon her, partly for the purpose of offering her their sympathy and partly with an intent to gratify their curiosity, ascertained, during the intervals of her hysterical spasms, that she cherished a wild and rather incoherent theory that Mr. Cowdrick had been brutally assassinated by some person and for some cause unknown. And this theory obtained some acceptance for a time among amiable people, who were disposed to take the most charitable view of the situation. But the number of these speedily diminished when the newspapers, a day or two later, revealed the result of an official examination of the affairs of Mr. Cowdrick's bank. The public then learned that that financial institution was rotten through and through; that Mr. Cowdrick and his partners in crime had not only used, for purposes of private speculation, the money of the depositors, but that they had stolen everything of value that had been committed to their care, and had left the bank an absolute, hopeless wreck, and reduced the innocent and unsuspicious stockholders to beggary.

The public excitement, of course, was great. Mrs. Cowdrick's friends neglected her. The rich and influential De Flukes actually insulted her by sending to recall an invitation to their reception that had been sent to her. As if Mrs. Cowdrick could have attended the reception at any rate! This was the cruellest thing of all, to Mrs. Cowdrick. She broke down completely and went to bed, where Leonie waited upon her to supply her with almost alarming quantities of camphor and smelling-salts.

As no traces of the fugitive could be found; as no one could testify to having seen him leave the city; and as the detective force, after following out without success any number of what they considered excellent clues, appeared to have relapsed into a normal condition of imbecility and indifference, the conclusion reached by many persons was, that Cowdrick had destroyed himself; and the energetic and enterprising coroner, McSorley, who had just been elected upon the Democratic ticket, went to work to drag all the rivers and creeks and ponds in the neighborhood.

Colonel Hoker, the editor of the *Crab*, the leading daily paper, advocated a dozen different theories in turn, and his indomitable reporters not only secured early and accurate reports of the condition of the bank, but they obtained expressions of opinion from at least thirty eminent citizens who really knew no more about the matter than other people, and they watched Cowdrick's house so closely, and were so successful in establishing confidential relations with the chambermaid, that they were able to tell how often the doctor called to see Mrs. Cowdrick, what quantity of reinvigorating drugs she consumed, how her medicine agreed with her, and what she had every day for dinner.

A country wherein a tyrant's power is used to shackle the press, and to rob it of freedom of utterance, does not know how much it misses.

The uncertainty in which the fate of Mr. Cowdrick was involved made it exceedingly difficult for Colonel Hoker to discuss the bank sensation in his editorial columns. If he could have felt sure that the unhappy fugitive had really slain himself, the course of the Colonel would have been clear; for then he could with safety have directed public attention to the peculiar atrocity of the transactions at the bank ; he could have held the miserable offender up before the public eye to point to him as an awful example to others, and especially to the young, and he could have preached many eloquent sermons upon the text, "Be sure your sins will find you out!"

But while a chance remained that Cowdrick was still alive and might return, the Colonel knew that it was the duty of persons upon whom it devolved to form public opinion through the instrumentality of the press, to be careful. He had learned from extended observation that an absent offender who has been roughly used as a warning against pursuance of the paths of vice, sometimes comes back, and, after gaining possession of power and riches, manifests a disposition to make things very uncomfortable for the eminent journalists who have used him as a basis for their denunciations of sin. And so the Colonel discussed the matter in the *Crab* only in a general way; lamenting the loss to the stockholders; expressing regret that "one of our most eminent citizens should be, for a time at least, in some respects under a cloud," and urging that perhaps the disaster might fairly be attributed to the spirit of wild speculation which seemed at times to animate entire communities, rather than to a deliberate purpose to inflict injury upon confiding and innocent persons.

The dexterity displayed by Colonel Hoker, in

keeping the Crab in such a nice position that while it apparently conceded much to public sentiment and the requirements of morality, it yet left a very wide margin for the contingency of Cowdrick's vindication and restoration to prosperity, was really marvellous.

But the nicest ingenuity sometimes will not avail against accident, or rather against that Fate which ordains catastrophe with ironical contempt for human foresight.

The Colonel was compelled to leave town for a few days, and in order to make the *Crab* entirely safe, he penned two editorial articles, one to be used in the event of the discovery of Cowdrick's dead body during his absence, the other to be inserted if Cowdrick should return alive to face his accusers and his fate.

The former article ran in this wise:—

"THE WAY OF THE TRANSGRESSOR.

"It has not often been our lot to present to our readers more striking proof than that which is found in our columns to-day of the fact that Satan makes hard bargains. It is now positively ascertained that Cowdrick the swindler, forger and thief, driven by desperation at the exposure of his awful crimes, and, let us hope, for the sake of human nature, by the stings of a conscience which could not hearken with indifference to the cries of the widows and orphans reduced at one fell blow to beggary, took his own life, and so ended a career of crime which honest men shrink from contemplating. It is, perhaps, for the best, however much we may regret that this wretched felon, burdened with guilt and shame, should have robbed the law of its right to punish, and should have gone into eternity unshriven, with the guilt of self-destruction added to the mountain of sins for which already he was required to give account. We shrink from discussion of the dreadful details of this shocking and sickening tragedy; but it will not have been enacted in vain if it shall seem to warn those who are tempted, as this man was, to surrender honesty at the demand of greed, and to permit the maddening thirst for gain to persuade them to trample in the dust their obligations to society, to their families, and to those who had given them their trust."

The second article pursued rather a different line of thought. It was to the following effect : —

"A Demand for Fair Play.

"We take a great deal of pleasure in announcing that Henry P. Cowdrick, Esq., the well-known banker, whose name has been before the public for some days past in connection with some unpleasant, but not yet positively authentic, rumors, has returned to the city in the enjoyment of excellent health. It is understood that an immediate further examination into the affairs of the bank will be made with the assistance of Mr. Cowdrick, and we merely express the general wish when we say that we hope to have some of the transactions that have excited severest comment explained in such a manner as to vindicate Mr. Cowdrick of every suspicion of wilful wrong-doing. Meantime, while this inquiry is pending, and while Mr. Cowdrick is preparing his statement of the case, it is only just to him to ask that there shall be a suspension of public opinion. His former high standing, his services to this community, the obscurity in which the recent operations of the bank are shrouded, and the most ordinary requirements of fair play, all combine to make it desirable that public opinion shall not pronounce a final verdict before the case is made up. We need not say how earnestly we trust that Mr. Cowdrick will emerge from his troubles with his honor unstained, and his reputation as a faithful guardian of the trusts confided to him, untarnished."

As a precautionary measure, the preparation of these articles appeared to be in a high sense judicious; and the Colonel naturally felt that the *Crab* might be depended on to keep nicely upon the right track until he should come home. But, alas! upon the next day but one after his departure, the foreman of the *Crab* composing-room, either mistaking his instructions, or being too much in haste in arranging his material, placed both articles together in the form, and the *Crab* came out in the morning to provoke the mirth of the town, to excite the contempt of its enemies, and to drive the unhappy associate editors of the paper to madness and despair. The manner in which the rival journals commented upon the occurrence was both brutal and infamous; and when the subject became a little stale, the editors of the rival journals put the *Crab* articles carefully away in scrap books, so as to make sure of having them ready for irritating and badgering Colonel Hoker upon every favorable opportunity during all the years to come.

The Colonel himself, upon discerning the catastrophe in a copy of the paper which he picked up at his hotel, expressed his feelings freely and vehemently by telegraph, and then he started home upon a fast express train for the purpose of explaining his views more fully and precisely.

The *Crab* itself alluded to the subject only so far as to suggest that the stupidity of an associate editor was accountable for the performance, and to hint that there was some reason for suspecting that bribery had been employed by the owners of rival papers, in the vain hope to bring the *Crab*, the only really infallible journal published, into contempt.

The efforts of McSorley, the coroner, to demonstrate the correctness of his theory of suicide were indefatigable. The body not having been discovered in any of the streams, McSorley began to search for it upon the land. The pursuit, however, was not profitable, for no traces of Mr. Cowdrick could be found. An ordinary coroner would have abandoned the hunt in despair; but McSorley was no common man. He brought to the performance of the functions of his office an enthusiasm which never failed to kindle at the promise of a fee; and as, in this case, he was thoroughly convinced that Cowdrick ought to have committed suicide, he felt that for Cowdrick to have evaded his duty in the matter would have been to perpetrate a wanton outrage upon Coroner McSorley.

The following extract from the local reports in the *Crab* will explain the character of the coroner's ultimate effort: —

"Yesterday a number of large bones were discovered beneath an old stable on Twelfth Street, by some laborers. It was believed by most of the spectators that they were the bones of a horse. But Coroner McSorley, who was sent for, declared at once his belief that they were portions of the skeleton of one of our prominent citizens, a banker, who has been missing for several days. This view was contested by several of the persons present upon the ground that the remains were absolutely fleshless, and manifestly very old. But the coroner, to demonstrate the accuracy of his view, proceeded to arrange the bones upon the pavement in the form of a man. He succeeded in the attempt to some extent, and was about to summon his jury of inquest, when Dr. Wattles came up. The doctor examined the skeleton, and then the following conversation ensued between him and Coroner McSorley: —

"'You don't imagine that to be the skeleton of a human being, do you, Mr. McSorley?'

"Certainly it is! Don't you see the shape of it?'

"'But, my dear sir, what you have arranged as the spine, runs clear up through what you suppose to be the skull, and projects two or three inches beyond the top of the head.'

"'Of course; and that is very likely the cause of all the trouble. The man's spine worked up into his head and disordered his mind. An aunt of mine, in Wisconsin, went mad from that very cause.'

"'But how do you account for the fact that there are three elbows in the left arm and none at all in the right.

"'Dr. Wattles, I am not obliged to account for eccentricities of formation in different individuals. I am satisfied with them as nature made them; and that is enough. It's none of my business if Cowdrick had eleven elbows in one arm, and thirty-four in the other.'

"'I will not argue the point, sir; but you certainly have no authority for locating two ribs in the neck, and for placing a row of teeth upon the upper side of the right foot. That foot, Mr. McSorley, is nothing but a fragment of a lower jawbone, depend upon it.'

"'How do you know that the deceased had no teeth there? You doctors always want to insist that every man is constructed on the same plan. I used to know a man in Canada who had four molar teeth in his ankle; and two of them were plugged. This appears to be a similar case.'

"'But you never knew a man who had a thighbone where his shoulder-blade ought to be, like this one, did you? You never saw a man with a knee-cap in the small of his back, either, did you?"

"'Maybe I did, and maybe I didn't. I have no time to discuss the subject now. The inquest that I am about to hold will bring out the facts. Mr. O'Flynn, swear in the jury!'"

The evidence that was given by the witnesses was of the most varied and entertaining character; and though much of it was vague and much was irrelevant, the jury appeared to have no ifficulty in reaching a conclusion, for, after a few minutes' deliberation, they brought in a verdict that "the deceased, Henry P. Cowdrick, came to his death from cause or causes unknown;" and then they collected their fees and dispersed, with a grateful consciousness that they had fully discharged their duty to society.

But, of course, perfectly disinterested persons, persons who were not in the way of earning jury fees, were disposed to regard with incredulity the conclusions reached by the coroner and his friends, and still it was for the community a vexed question — What had become of Mr. Cowdrick?

The coroner's theory, however, was not entirely forgotten, because Dr. Wattles sent to one of the daily papers a communication, in which he expressed his opinion of the bones over which the inquest was held. This provoked from "An Eminent Scientist," who had not seen the bones, a suggestion of the possibility that they may have belonged to some mysterious creature who was the missing link between man and the lower orders of mammalia.

To this there came a hot response from Father Tunicle and several other clergymen, who proceeded to show the monstrous folly and wickedness of such a supposition, and who demonstrated that Science and Infidelity, not to say sheer Paganism, were pretty nearly one and the same thing.

The clerical utterances so excited at least half-a-dozen other Eminent Scientists that the latter undertook to demonstrate, through the columns of the daily papers, that the book of Genesis was written by Jeremiah; that life first visited this planet in the shape of star-dust, which, after developing into jelly-fish, gradually grew to the ape form, and

"You never saw a Man with a Knee-cap in the Small of his Back." Page 159.

ultimately became man. They showed how all religion is priestcraft and superstition; they traced all the creeds backward to myths built upon the operations of Nature; they could hardly refrain from mirth at the notion of a Great First Cause; and they positively refused to join with the multitude, for whom, however, they expressed deep compassion, in believing anything that they could not see, or feel, or analyze.

It seemed a large controversy to grow out of Coroner McSorley's arrangement of the unearthed bones; but the controversialists manifestly regarded it as of the very highest importance; although, when it was ended, each believed precisely what he had believed before.

At St. Cadmus's, the Cowdrick tragedy had had, upon the whole, rather a good effect. The event was mournful, of course, but it produced some desirable results. The Tunicle party felt that they had lost one of their most ardent supporters, and a contributor upon whose wealth they had depended greatly for the success of their plans. Thus they were able more easily to perceive the excellence of a spirit of concession, and at once they began to approach the other side with offers of compromise.

Happily, at this juncture, Father Krum received a "call" to a church in another diocese, and he accepted it promptly, sending in his resignation of his position as the assistant minister at St. Cadmus's. Father Tunicle, then, of his own motion, offered to abandon, as not absolutely essential to salvation, the use of black book-markers upon Good Friday; whereupon Mr. Yetts and his adherents in the vestry declared themselves satisfied, and once more resumed their accustomed places in the sanctuary on Sunday.

Upon the second Sunday after the disappearance of Mr. Cowdrick, Father Tunicle, who held stoutly to the theory that his late vestryman had been murdered, resolved to refer indirectly in his remarks from the pulpit to the bereavement; and upon his invitation, Mrs. Cowdrick and Leonie attended the church, heavily veiled, to obtain what consolation might be possible from the services.

Father Tunicle, being somewhat pressed for time during the preceding week, had procured from a dealer in such commodities, at the price of three dollars, an original sermon addressed to persons in affliction, and this he brought with him into the pulpit, wrapped in Leonie's worked velvet sermon-cover. The fact that the sermon was nicely lithographed, so that it closely resembled manuscript, made it quite impossible for any one to suspect that it was not the product of Father Tunicle's own intellectual effort and of his earnest sympathy. The discourse was divided into four parts; three heads, and an affecting application; which, at three dollars for the whole, of course amounted to just seventy-five cents a part — not too much, surely, for so wholesome and comforting a sermon.

Father Tunicle preached it with much eloquence; but Mrs. Cowdrick, despite an occasional sob beneath her veil, managed to restrain her feelings until Father Tunicle had gotten through with one dollar and a half's worth of the sermon, and had begun upon the third head. Then Mrs. Cowdrick could stand it no longer. One passionate outburst of grief followed another, until, when the attention of the entire congregation was directed to Mrs. Cowdrick, the sexton came in, and led her in a fainting condition down the aisle to the door, where she was placed in the carriage with Leonie, with nothing to solace her but the reflection that everybody in the church, including the odious De Flukes, *must* have noticed her seal-skin sacque and her lovely diamond earrings.

CHAPTER IV.

MR. WEEMS. — TOM BENNET'S WAY. — MR. GUNN'S
PROPOSAL.—BREACH OF PROMISE.—THE TRIAL.

ONE morning, Mr. Julius Weems sat in his studio, dressed in velvet working jacket and slouching hat. With palette on thumb, brush in hand, and pipe in mouth, Mr. Weems was endeavoring to give a sufficiently aged appearance to a " Saul and Witch of Endor," by Salvator Rosa.

" Hang it," said Mr. Weems to himself, as he placed a dab of burnt umber on the withered cheek of the hag, "everything seems to go wrong! It was bad enough to have old Cowdrick dupe me in the way he did; but right on top of that, to hear from Crook and Gudgem that the Rubens business is being overdone, and that they have had eight St. Ethelbertas offered to them during the week, is a little too much. If the entire profession of artists is going to turn to painting old masters, I will have to come down to modern art and poor prices. It's the worst luck! There is no chance at all for a man to earn an honest living!"

Mr. Weems's soliloquy was interrupted by a light knocking upon his door. Hastily throwing a cloth over the picture upon his easel, and turning two Titians and a Raphael with their faces to the wall, Mr. Weems opened the door and admitted the visitor.

"Good morning!" said the intruder. "Don't know me, I suppose?"

"No." responded Mr. Weems.

."My name is Gunn; Benjamin P. Gunn."

"I have heard of you. You are interested in life assurance, I believe? A canvasser, or something?"

"Yes, I was; but I have given that up now. The business was overdone. I grew tired of it!"

"You don't know anything, then, about Mr. Cowdrick's case? I mean whether he had much on his life or not?"

"Oh! well, I have heard that he was insured for fifty thousand or so; I don't remember the exact amount. But it makes no difference."

"Will the widow be likely to get it if he is dead?"

"In my opinion she will have a mighty slim chance of collecting anything, even if she can prove that he is actually deceased. From what I know of the President of the Widows' and Orphans' Mutual Life Insurance Company, I believe he will fight the claim through all the courts. That is his rule. Nearly all the companies do it."

" What! even if it is a clear case for the policy-holder?"

" Of course! That is the regular thing. They'll worry a widow so that she will be glad to compromise on half the claim, and by the time she has paid her lawyers most of that is gone."

" That seems hard!"

" Yes; that is one of the reasons why I quit. Take the case of Lemuel A. Gerlach, for example. You remember it?"

" No."

" Well, sir, I did my best to persuade that man to insure. He didn't want to; but I harried him into it. I waited on him at his office; I disturbed him at his meals; I lay in wait for him when he came home from the club; I followed him to the sea-shore in summer; when he went yachting I pursued him with a steam-tug; when he was sick I got the apothecary to enclose our circulars with his medicine; I sat next to him in church for four consecutive Sundays, and slipped mortality tables into his prayer-book; I rode with him in the same carriage when he went to funerals, and lectured him all the way out to the cemetery upon the uncertainty of human life. Finally, he succumbed. I knew he would. It was only a question of time. I took him down to the office; the company's surgeon examined him, and said he was the healthiest man he ever saw — not a flaw in him anywhere. So he paid his premium and got his policy. Two months later he died. When Mrs. Gerlach called to get her money, the President threatened to have her put out of the office because she denied that Gerlach's liver was torpid when he took out his policy."

"Did they pay, finally?"

"Pay! not a dollar! The widow sued to recover, and the company put the surgeon and eight miscellaneous doctors on the stand to prove that Gerlach for years had been a complete physical wreck, with more diseases than most people ever heard of; and they undertook to show that Gerlach had devoted the latter part of his life to organizing a scheme for foisting himself upon the company for the purpose of swindling it. That was five years ago. The case is pending in the courts yet, and the widow has already spent twenty per cent. more than the face of the policy."

"It was not a very profitable speculation, certainly."

"No, sir; it wasn't. I'll tell you what, Mr. Weems, if a man wants to realize on his departed relatives, that is not the way to do it. Anything is better than life insurance; even Tom Bennet's way."

"How was that?"

"Why, Tom Bennet, you know, is a friend of mine, who lives out in Arkansas. And one day, some years ago, a little cemetery in the town in which he lived was sold out by the sheriff. Tommy was looking about for a site on which to build a house for himself, and, as this one happened to suit him, he bid on it, and got it at a very low figure. When he began to dig the cellar, Tom found that the folks who were interred in the place had been petrified, to a man. Every occupant turned to solid stone! So Tom, you know, being a practical kind of man, made up his mind to quarry out the departed, and to utilize them for building material."

"Rather unkind, wasn't it?"

"Tom didn't appear to think so. And as the building made progress, he rubbed down Mr. Flaherty for a door-sill, and had Judge Paterson chipped off with a chisel into the handsomest hitching-post that you ever saw."

"Horrible!"

"Yes. Some of the McTurk family were put into the bow-window, between the sashes, and the whole of the families of Major Magill and Mr. Dougherty were worked into the foundation. And when the roof was going on, Tom Bennet took General Hidenhooper, and bored a flue through the crown of his head downward, so as to use him for a chimney-top. The edifice, when completed, presented a rather striking appearance."

"What did the surviving relatives have to say?"

"They were indignant, of course; but as the courts decided that the petrifactions, without doubt, were part of the real estate, and were included in the title-deeds, they could do nothing but remonstrate, and Tom paid no attention to that."

"Then it is your professional opinion," said Mr. Weems, returning to the subject uppermost in his mind, "that the Insurance Company will not pay, even if Mr. Cowdrick be found to be dead!"

Mr. Gunn smiled in a peculiar manner, and then, after a moment's hesitation, he said: "Really, you know, Mr. Weems, there is no use of discussing that contingency. Cowdrick is not dead."

"How do you know?"

"Why, that is the very thing I called to see you about. I am on the detective force now. Regularly employed by the police authorities. I know exactly where Cowdrick is, and I have had him under surveillance from the very first day that he left home."

"Why haven't you arrested him, then?"

Mr. Gunn laughed. "Oh, it was not worth while. I knew I could get him whenever I wanted him. It never pays to be in a hurry with such matters."

"A heavy reward has been offered for him, I believe," said Mr. Weems.

"That's just it," replied Mr. Gunn.

"I don't understand you."

"Why, the authorities express their anxiety to catch him, by offering to pay five hundred dollars to accomplish the feat. Now, the question is, will Cowdrick's friends express their wish that he shall not be caught, by going a little higher, say up to one thousand dollars?"

"But I cannot imagine why you should come to me with such a proposition. Why don't you go to Mrs. Cowdrick?"

"I'd rather deal with a man; a man understands business so much better. And as you are interested in Cowdrick's family, going, as it were, to be near and dear to him, it struck me that maybe you might give him a chance to go off quietly upon a trip to Europe, or somewhere, and save him from a term of years in jail. How does it strike you?"

"Very unfavorably. In the first place, I have not enough money for your purpose; and, in the second place, if I did have it, I should decline to expend it for the benefit of Mr. Cowdrick."

"Then you refuse to negotiate?"

"Yes, positively."

"Very well," said Mr. Detective Gunn, rising, "I merely wished to ascertain what your views were. Pardon me for interrupting you. No offence, I hope? Good morning." And Mr. Gunn withdrew, while Weems closed and bolted the door.

The artist had hardly seated himself, and resumed the work of depicting the Witch of Endor, when another visitor knocked at the door. Mr. Weems arose, drew the bolt, and opened the door wide enough to permit him to look out.

"May I come in?" asked Leonie Cowdrick, with an effort at cheeriness in her voice.

"Oh, certainly. Glad to see you," replied Mr. Weems, admitting her. But Mr. Weems did not look as if he really felt very glad.

"Pardon me for calling, Julius," she said, "but I think I must have left my satchel when I was here last week. I cannot find it anywhere."

Poor thing! Any excuse would have sufficed to account for her coming to try to discover why it was that her lover had not visited her for nearly a week.

"I do not think it is here," said Mr. Weems; "I am sure it is not, or I should have seen it."

"Then it is lost beyond recovery," exclaimed Leonie, sinking into a chair, and fanning herself, while she looked very hard at the artist, who pretended to be busy with his picture.

"Haven't heard anything from your father yet, I suppose?" said Mr. Weems, after a painful interval of silence.

"Nothing; absolutely nothing. Poor mother is nearly distracted. We are in great trouble. And I thought, Julius, you would have been with us more during this trial."

"Well," said Mr. Weems, "you see I have been so very busy, and I have had so many engagements, that I could not find time enough to call very frequently."

"It looked almost like neglect," said Leonie, sadly. "I could hardly bear it." And she put her handkerchief to her eyes.

"Confound it!" said Mr. Weems to himself, "now there is going to be a scene."

"Mother said she could hardly believe that you really loved me," continued Leonie.

"She said that, did she?" asked Mr. Weems, somewhat bitterly. "Did she ask you if you really loved *me?*"

"No, Julius; she knows that I do. You know it, too."

"Love," said the artist, "means faith, trust, fair play, and candor, among other things, I have always thought."

"What do you mean by that, Julius?"

"Well, I don't want to be unkind, Leonie; but do you think that a woman who truly loved a man would misrepresent her age to him; or that she would be absolutely silent respecting previous engagements that she had contracted? How do I know that you care more for me than you did for Baxter and the others?"

"Mr. Weems," exclaimed Leonie, indignantly, "this is cruel. It is worse, — it is shameful. You seem to have known all there was to know, without seeking information from me."

"That is what made it so very painful," replied Mr. Weems, trying to look as if his feelings had experienced a terrible wrench. "It was dreadful to learn from outside sources what I should have heard from your own lips. When a woman pretends to give me her heart, I expect her to give me her confidence also."

"Pretends!" exclaimed Leonie, rising. "Pretends! What do you mean, sir, by 'pretends'! Do you dare to insinuate that I deliberately deceived you?"

"Well," said Mr. Weems, calmly, "that is perhaps a rather violent construction of my language; but we will not quarrel over phrases."

"I did not think," said Leonie, tearfully but vehemently, "that I should be insulted when I came here, — insulted in the midst of my grief. It is unmanly, sir! It is cowardly! It is infamous!"

"I am sorry that you take that view of it. I did not intend to be discourteous, I am sure. Pray pardon me if I was so. It is clear, however, that, after what has passed, we can hardly sustain our former relation to each other."

"I understand you, sir," replied Leonie, scornfully; "I fully realize your meaning. You intended at the outset to break our engagement. Well, sir, it is broken. I am glad to break it. I regard you with scorn and contempt. Hereafter we shall be as strangers to each other."

"I submit to your decision," returned the artist. "But — but, of course, you will return my letters?"

Leonie laughed a wild and bitter laugh, and, gathering up her skirts as if she feared contamination, she swept haughtily from the room, without speaking another word.

"That is settled, at any rate! said Mr. Weems, as he closed the door. "That is just what I wanted. I can't afford to marry poverty. But it is a bad business about those letters of mine! I wonder if she intends to use them against me?" And Mr. Weems, relighting his pipe, sat down in his easy-chair to make a mental review of the situation.

Mr. Weems was not permitted to remain long in doubt respecting the intentions of Miss Cowdrick. Upon the very next day he received from Messrs. Pullock and Shreek, attorneys, formal notice that Miss Leonie Cowdrick had authorized them to bring a suit against him for breach of promise of marriage, the claim for pecuniary damages being laid at thirty thousand dollars.

Mr. Weems regarded the proceeding with not a little alarm; but, upon consulting his lawyer, Mr. Porter, and detailing to him the conversation between the artist and Leonie at the time of the rupture, Mr. Weems was assured that he could make an excellent defence upon the theory that the lady had broken the engagement; and he was strongly advised to permit the case to go to trial.

It did so right speedily; for the attorneys for the plaintiff secured for it an early place upon the list, and they manifested a disposition to push the defendant in the most unmerciful manner permitted by the law.

When the case was called for trial, Mr. Weems's lawyer moved for a postponement; and he pleaded, argued, fought, and begged for his motion as if the life of his client and his own happiness were staked upon a brief delay. As Mr. Weems was quite ready to proceed, he could not imagine why there should be such earnest contention respecting this point. But, of course, it was the regular professional thing to do. Mr. Weems's lawyer did not really want a continuance. He merely cared to put himself right upon the record by conducting the performance in the customary manner.

Messrs. Pullock and Shreek, counsel for the plaintiff, resisted the motion vigorously. When Mr. Shreek arose to address the court, with regard to it, the unpractised spectator would have supposed that the learned counsel was amazed as well as shocked at the conduct of the defence in asking that the arm of justice should be stayed, even for a week, from visiting punishment upon the monster who was now called to answer for his offences. It seemed really to grieve Mr. Shreek, to distress and hurt him, that the counsel for the defence, a member of an honorable profession, and a man who, upon ordinary occasions, had the respect of society and the confidence of his fellow-creatures, should so far set at defiance all considerations of propriety, all sense of what was due to the lovely sufferer who came here for protection and redress, and all the demands of justice, honor, and decency, as to try to keep the hideous facts of this case even for a time from the attention of an intelligent and sympathetic jury.

Mr. Shreek, as he brought his remarks to a close, was so deeply moved by the scandalous nature of the conduct of counsel for the defence, that Mr. Weems was disposed to believe that the breach between them was final and irreparable ; but a moment later, when Judge Winker decided that the trial must proceed at once, Mr. Weems was surprised to perceive his lawyer and Mr. Shreek chatting and laughing together precisely as if Mr. Shreek had not regarded Mr. Porter's behavior with mingled horror and disgust.

In selecting the jurymen, the manifest purpose of the lawyers upon both sides was to reject every man of ordinary intelligence, and to prefer the persons who seemed, from their appearance, least likely to possess the power of reaching a rational conclusion upon any given subject. And when the jury had been obtained, Mr. Weems, looking at them, thought that he had never, in all his life, seen twelve more stupid-looking men.

Leonie Cowdrick came in as the case opened, and took a seat close by Mr. Pullock. She was dressed with exquisite taste, and Mr. Weems was really surprised to perceive that she seemed quite pretty.

Her face was partly covered by a veil, and in her hand she carried a kerchief, with which occasionally she gently touched her eyes.

It was clear enough that Mr. Pullock had her in training for the purpose of producing effects upon the jury, for whenever during the proceedings anything of a pathetic nature was developed, Mr. Pullock signalled her, and at once her handkerchief went to her face.

The trial endured through two days, and much of the time was occupied by wrangles, squabbles, and fierce recriminations between the lawyers, who, after working themselves into furious passion, and seeming ready to fall upon each other and tear each other to pieces, invariably resumed their friendly intercourse during the recesses, and appeared ready to forgive and forget all the injuries of the past.

One of the jurymen was asleep during the larger portion of the sessions upon both days; two others paid no attention to the evidence, but persistently gaped about the court-room, and the remainder seemed to consider the quarrels between the counsel as the only matters of genuine importance in the case. During the first day Mr. Detective Gunn came in, and seeing Mr. Weems, went over to whisper in his ear that Cowdrick had been arrested, and would reach town upon the morrow.

"We had to take the reward," said Gunn. "Not one of his friends would give any more. It's a pity for the old man, too! I see well enough now why *you* wouldn't lend a hand." And Mr. Gunn looked toward Leonie, and laughed.

When Mr. Porter was not engaged in examining or cross-examining a witness, he addressed his attention to the task of getting upon terms of jolly good-fellowship with the members of the jury who remained awake. He sat near to the foreman, and he was continually passing jokes to that official, with the back of his hand to his mouth — jokes which the foreman manifestly relished, for he always sent them further along in the jury-box.

This mirthfulness appeared to have a very depressing effect upon Mr. Pullock, for whenever he observed it he assumed a look of deep mournfulness, as if it distressed him beyond measure that any one should have an impulse to indulge in levity in the presence of the unutterable woe which had made the life of his fair but heart-broken client simply a condition of hopeless misery. And while the reckless jurymen laughed, Mr. Pullock would shake his head sadly, seeming to feel as if Justice had expanded her wings and fled forever from the tribunals of man; and then he would nudge the lovely victim by his side, as a hint for her to hoist her handkerchief as another signal to the jury that she was in distress.

But Mr. Porter's humor, brutal and unfeeling though it might be, could not be restrained. Particularly did many of the points in the evidence offered by the plaintiff impress him ludicrously; and at times, when Mr. Shreek was developing what he evidently regarded as a fact of high and solemn importance, Mr. Porter would wink at the foreman, and begin to writhe upon his chair in his efforts to restrain himself from violating the decorum of the Temple of Justice by bursting into uproarious laughter.

These rather scandalous attempts to convey to the jurymen who were awake Mr. Porter's theory that the testimony for the prosecution was nonsense of the most absurd description, and to impress them with the belief that when Mr. Porter's turn came, he would knock it, so to speak, higher than a kite, provoked Mr. Shreek to such an extent, that, finally, he stopped short in his examination of a witness, to snarl out to Mr. Porter:—

"What are you laughing at? I don't notice anything in the testimony that is so very funny!"

"The muscles of my face are my own," rejoined Mr. Porter, "and I will use them as I please."

"But you have no right to divert the attention of the jury by your buffoonery!" replied Mr. Shreek, angrily.

"I will laugh when, and how, and at what I please," said Mr. Porter. "I shall not accept any dictation from you. It's not my fault if you have a ridiculous case!"

"I will show you how ridiculous it is before I get through," answered Mr. Shreek.

"I know all about it already!" said Mr. Porter.

Then Mr. Shreek proceeded with his examination, and Mr. Porter laughed almost out loud two or three times, merely to show the jury that he regarded Mr. Shreek's remonstrance with positive contempt. But it must be confessed that Mr. Porter's mirthfulness, in this instance, seemed to lack heartiness and spontaneity.

But when Mr. Porter's turn came to address the jury, his sense of humor had become completely benumbed, while that of Mr. Shreek had undergone really abnormal development; for Mr. Porter could hardly attempt to plunge into pathos, or to permit his unfettered imagination to take a little flight, without Mr. Shreek's humorous susceptibilities being aroused in such a manner that the closure of his mouth with his handkerchief alone prevented him from offending the dignity of the Court.

Mr. Porter's appeal to the jury in behalf of his client was based upon his asseveration that this was the most intelligent jury that he had ever had the honor of addressing, and upon his solemn conviction that the jurymen not only represented accurately the most respectable portion of the community, but that, as upon this occasion the jury system itself was upon trial to prove whether it truly was the bulwark of liberty, that barrier against injustice and oppression which it was vaunted to be, so this jury were, it might be said, called upon to determine whether the system was to retain the respect and confidence of mankind or to be branded by public sentiment as a wretched failure, and to be regarded in the future by all honorable men with loathing and contempt.

As two of the jurymen happened to be Irishmen, and one of them was a member of the Odd Fellows' Society, Mr. Porter did not neglect to allude to the circumstance that Mr. Weems's great-grandfather was born in Ireland; and the learned counsel took occasion to speak with indignant warmth of the wrongs that have been endured by Ireland, and to express his deep sympathy with her unfortunate and suffering people.

Of the noble aims and splendid achievements of the Odd Fellows' Society, it was hardly necessary for Mr. Porter to speak at length. He could never hope to command language of sufficient force to explain his appreciation of the services rendered to Society by this invaluable organization; but the fact that both he and his client had for years belonged to the sacred brotherhood, to which they gave their energies and their devotion, was a sufficient guarantee of the strength of their affection for it.

In concluding, Mr. Porter merely desired to direct the attention of the gentlemen of the jury to the fact that if designing women were to be permitted to decoy unsuspecting men into contracts of marriage merely for the purpose of securing by artful means repudiation of the contract, so that the ground would be laid for a demand for money, then no man was safe, and no one could tell at what moment he might fall into a snare laid for him by an unprincipled adventuress. Mr. Porter then expressed his entire confidence in the intention of the jury to give a verdict for his client, and he sat down with a feeling that he had discharged his duty in an effective manner.

Mr. Shreek, in reply, observed that he should begin with the assertion that in two particulars this was one of the most remarkable cases that it had ever been his fortune to try. In the first place, he was unable to refer to an occasion, during more than twenty years' experience at the bar, when he had had the honor of addressing a jury so intelligent and so worthy of being entrusted with interests of the very highest character as this one was; and never had he felt so much confidence as he now felt when he came before these highly-cultivated, keenly sagacious, and thoroughly representative gentlemen to ask for justice, simple justice, for an unhappy woman. In the second place, while it had fallen to his lot to witness more than one painful and repulsive scene, more than one example of the capacity of human beings for reaching the deepest depths of degradation, in their efforts to rob Justice of her own, and to make her very name a byword and a reproach among the wise and the good, he had never yet received so violent a shock as that which came to him to-day, when, with mortification and grief, he had heard a member of the bar, sworn to seek to uphold the sanctity of the law and the honor of a proud profession, not only misrepresent the truth most villanously, but so far forget his manhood as to stoop to insult, to revile, to smite with a ribald and envenomed tongue, a fair and noble woman, who already bent beneath an awful load of domestic sorrow, and whose only fault was that she had come here to seek redress for an injury the depth of which no tongue could tell, the agony of which the imagination of him who has not fathomed all the mystery of a woman's love could never hope to realize. He would only say, in dismissing this most distressing and humiliating portion of the subject, that he left the offender to the punishment of a conscience which, hardened and seared though it was, still must have in store for him pangs of remorse of which he, Mr. Shreek, trembled to think.

The learned counsel for the plaintiff asked the gentlemen of the jury to review with him the facts of the case, as presented to them by the evidence.

Already they knew something of the trustfulness and confidence of woman's nature; their experience within the sacred privacy of the domestic circle had taught them that when a woman gave her affection, she gave it wholly, never doubting, never suspecting, that the object of it might be unworthy to wear so priceless a jewel. Such a creature, — the peerless being of whom the poet had eloquently said, that Earth was a Desert, Eden was a Wild, Man was a Savage, until Woman smiled — was peculiarly exposed to the wiles of artful and unscrupulous men, who, urged by those Satanic impulses which appear in some men as unquestionable proof of the truthfulness of the Scriptural theory of demoniac possession, should attempt to gain the prize only to trample it ruthlessly in the dust.

In this instance the destroyer came to find a pure and beautiful love, with its tendrils ready to cling fondly to some dear object. By honeyed phrases, by whispered vows so soon to be falsified, by tender glances from eyes which revealed none of the desperate wickedness of the soul within, by all the arts and devices employed upon such occasions, the defendant had persuaded those tendrils to cling to him, to entwine about him. Artless, unsophisticated, unlearned in the ways of the sinful world, the beautiful plaintiff had listened and believed; and for a few short weeks she was happy in the fond belief that this reptile who had crawled across the threshold of her maiden's heart was a prince of men, an idol whom she might worship with unstinted adoration.

But she was soon to be undeceived. Choosing the moment when her natural defender was absent, when his coward's deed could be done without the infliction of condign punishment from him who loved this his only child far better than his life, the defendant, scoffing at the holiest of the emotions, despising the precious treasure confided to his keeping, and gloating over the misery inflicted wantonly and savagely by his too brutal hand, cast off her love, closed his ears to her sighs, observed unmoved the anguish of her soul, and flung her aside, heart-broken and despairing, while he passed coldly on to seek new hearts to break, new lives to blast and ruin, new victims to dupe and decoy with his false tongue and his vile hypocrisy.

In support of his assertions, Mr. Shreek proposed to read to the jury some of the letters addressed by the defendant to the plaintiff, while still he maintained an appearance of fidelity to her; and the jury would perceive more clearly than ever the blackness of the infamy which characterized the defendant's conduct, when at last he showed himself in his true colors.

Mr. Shreek then produced a bundle of letters, which had been placed in evidence ; and when he did so, the newspaper reporters sharpened their pencils, the somnolent juryman awoke, the judge laid down his pen to listen. Leonie again wiped her eyes, and the crowd of spectators made a buzz, which indicated their expectation that they were going to hear something of an uncommonly interesting nature.

Mr. Weems alone seemed wholly sad.

Mr. Shreek would first invite the attention of the jury to a letter, dated simply "Tuesday morning," and signed with the name of the defendant. It was as follows : —

"MY SWEET ROSEBUD" (laughter from the spectators), — " Before me lies your darling little letter of yesterday. I have read it over and over again, and kissed it many times." (Merriment in the court-room.) "Why do you wish that you had wings, that you might fly away and be at rest ? " ("No wonder she wanted wings," interjected Mr. Shreek.) "Am I not all you wish ? ". ("He didn't seem to be," said Mr. Shreek.) "Cannot I make you perfectly happy? Oh, how I love you, my sweet, pretty, charming Rosebud! You are all in all to me. I think I can look down the dim vista of time, and see you going with me hand-in-hand through all the long and happy years." ("He was not quite so short-sighted as he appears to be," said Mr. Shreek ; whereupon there was general laughter. Even Leonie laughed a little.)

"And now, my own sweet love" (laughter), "I must bid you good-night. I send you a thousand kisses from your own, ever constant JULIUS."

"Rosebud! gentlemen," said Mr. Shreek, as he folded the letter away and took out another. "Yes, a rosebud, and he the vile canker-worm that was eating away its life! But this is only one of many such effusions. Upon another occasion, he says:

"MY BIRDIE," (general laughter,)—"This morning a blessing came to me by the hands of the postman, and what do you think? the writer did not sign her name, and I am not sure whom I should thank, but I am going to risk thanking you, my own dear, loving Leonie. Why do you call me an angel, darling?" ("That," observed Mr. Shreek, "was enough to astonish him!" And then everybody laughed again.) "I am only a plain, prosy man," ("A close shave to the truth," said Mr. Shreek,) "but I am exalted by having your love. If I were an angel, I would hover over you, my sweet," ("And very likely drop something on her," added Mr. Shreek,) "and protect you. You ask me if I think of you often! Think of you, Leonie! I think of nothing else." (Laughter.) "You are always in my mind; and if I keep on loving you more and more, as I am doing, I shall die with half my love untold." (Laughter. "Wonderful how he loved her, wasn't it?" remarked Mr. Shreek.) "Again I send you a million kisses" (merriment), "and a fond good-night, and pleasant dreams.
"Your adoring J."

"Observe," said Mr. Shreek, taking out still another letter, "how he mocked her! How hollow, how infamous all of that sounds, in view of his subsequent treachery!"

Here Miss Cowdrick bowed her head and wept, and Mr. Weems looked as if he felt that death at the stake would be mere pastime in comparison with this experience.

"We now come," said Mr. Shreek, "to letter number three — a document which reveals this moral monster in even a more hideous light."

"MY PRECIOUS ONE" (great laughter) — "How can I ever thank you for the trouble you have taken to make me those lovely slippers? They are two sizes too small for me" (laughter); "but I can look at them and kiss them" ("He was a tremendous kisser in his way, you observe," said the learned counsel), "and think of you meantime. I could not come to see you last evening, for I sprained my ankle; but I looked at your picture and kissed it" (laughter. "At it again, you see," said Mr. Shreek); "and I read over your old letters. There is a knock at my door now, and I must stop. But I will say, I love you. Oh, how I love you! my life and my light.   Fondly your own   JULIUS."

"But," continued the eloquent counsel for the plaintiff, "this false lover, this maker of vows that were as idle as the whispering of the summer wind, did not always write prose to the unhappy lady whom he had deceived. Sometimes he breathed out his bogus affection through the medium of verse. Sometimes he invoked the sacred Muse to help him to shatter the heart of this loving and trustful woman. With the assistance of a rhyming dictionary, or perhaps having, with a bold and lawless hand, filched his sweets from some true poet who had felt the impulses of a genuine passion, he wrote and sent to my lovely but unfortunate client the following lines:

> "Sweetheart, if I could surely choose
> The aptest word in passion's speech" —

"That," said the counsel, "indicates that he would steal his poetry if he could."

> "And all its subtlest meaning use,
> With eloquence your soul to teach;
> Still, forced by its intensity,
> Sweetheart, my love would voiceless be!"

(Laughter.)
"And heartless, as well as voiceless," added the counsel.

> "Sweetheart, though all the days and hours
> Sped by, with love in sharpest stress,
> To find some reach of human powers,
> Its faintest impulse to express,
> Till Time merged in Eternity,
> Sweetheart, my love would voiceless be!"

(Roars of laughter.)

Mr. Shreek declared that he would read no more. It made his heart sick — professionally, of course — to peruse these revolting evidences of man's inhumanity to lovely woman; of the amazing perfidy of the plaintiff, Weems. This voiceless lover, who was not only voiceless, but shameless, feelingless, and merciless as well, was now before them, arraigned by that law whose foremost function was to protect the weak, and to punish those who assail the helpless. It rests with you, gentlemen, to say whether the cry for help made to that law by this desolate woman with the lacerated heart shall be made in vain. So far as Mr. Shreek was concerned, he felt perfectly certain that the jury would award to his client the full amount of damages — a miserable recompense, at the best — for which she sued.

The judge's charge was very long, very dull, and full of the most formidable words, phrases, and references. Those who were able to follow it intelligently, however, perceived that it really amounted to nothing more than this : If you find the defendant guilty, it is your duty to bring in a verdict to that effect; while, upon the other hand, if you find him not guilty, you are required to acquit him.

At six o'clock in the evening the jury retired, and the court waited for the verdict. At six-thirty, the jury sent to ask that the love-letters might be given to them; and it was whispered about that one of the jurymen had obtained the impression, somehow, that they were written by Miss Cowdrick to Weems. At a quarter past seven, the jury wanted to know if they could have cigars; and Mr. Porter sent them a couple of bundles at his own expense. At eight, word came out that one of the jurymen, evidently the slumberer, wanted a question of fact cleared up: Was the man suing the woman, or the woman the man? This having been settled, the court waited until half past eight, when, amid much excitement, the jury came in, and disappointed everybody with the announcement that it was quite impossible for them to agree.

Mr. Porter whispered to Mr. Weems that there was an Irishman upon that jury whom he felt confident of from the first.

The judge went over the case again briefly, but learnedly and vaguely, and sent the jury back. At nine o'clock the jury came into court a second time, and presented a verdict of guilty, imposing damages to the amount of five thousand dollars.

There was an outburst of applause; Leonie leaned her head upon the breast of Mr. Pullock, and wept from mingled feelings of joy and grief. Mr. Shreek observed to Mr. Porter, that "this is all we ever expected;" and Mr. Porter said to Weems that he was lucky to get off so easily; for he, Porter, had anticipated a much worse result.

Poor Weems alone seemed to regard the verdict with less than perfect satisfaction; and he was no better pleased next morning, when Colonel Hoker's *Crab* and all the other papers came out with reports of the trial in flaring type, and with the entire batch of love-letters, poetry and all, in full.

The journals also contained an announcement that Mr. Cowdrick had been captured and brought home, and had at once been released upon bail.

CHAPTER V.

MR. COWDRICK'S RETURN. — MR. WEEMS TAKES A NEW VIEW OF HIS POSITION. — JUSTICE.

R. COWDRICK again sat in his easy-chair, in his library, before the sham fire, and with him sat his wife and daughter. They were talking of the trial of Mr. Cowdrick, which was to begin on the morrow.

"It is very disagreeable, of course," said Mr. Cowdrick; "but in this life we have to take the bitter with the sweet."

"But, oh, papa," said Leonie, "how dreadful it will be if the verdict goes against you. Do you think they would actually send a man of your position to a horrid prison?"

"Leonie!" exclaimed Mrs. Cowdrick, "I am surprised at your speaking of such things. Pray don't do it again. My nerves will not stand it."

"You need not be alarmed, my dear child," said Mr. Cowdrick, smiling. "My friends have arranged things comfortably for me with the prosecuting attorney, and the other authorities. I had an offer made to me to have the jury packed in my interest, but I was assured that it was unnecessary, and, besides, I felt that it would perhaps be wrong for me to descend to corruption."

"It is a terrible experience at the best," said Mrs. Cowdrick; "but there is some satisfaction in the reflection that we are not reduced to absolute poverty."

"That is my greatest consolation," rejoined Mr. Cowdrick. "Pinyard tells me that I may count on saving at least two hundred and fifty thousand dollars from the wreck; invested in good securities, too."

"Then we can go to a watering-place, next summer, as usual?" asked Leonie.

"Yes, dear."

"And can we keep our carriage and our servants, and everything, just as before?"

"Certainly; there will be no difference."

Leonie reflected for a moment, and then sighed heavily.

"And I think very likely," said Mr. Cowdrick, "that my poor little girl can have her lover back again, if she wants him, too."

"Papa, what do you mean?" asked Leonie.

"Why, I commissioned a man named Gunn, in whom I have some confidence, to visit Weems, and to sound him, to ascertain how he felt with regard to the result of your suit."

"Well?"

"Gunn reports to me that Weems feels repentant; says he always loved you, and would give anything to have the past recalled."

Here Mr. Cowdrick, having constructed a sturdy falsehood, winked at his wife; and Leonie said:

"Well, papa, I don't know whether I am quite willing to forgive him, but I confess that I care more for Julius than for any other person."

"We shall see what can be done," remarked Mr. Cowdrick. "And now you must excuse me. I have to go to meet my counsel to prepare for the trial;" and Mr. Cowdrick withdrew.

The interview between Mr. Weems and Mr. Benjamin P. Gunn, to which Mr. Cowdrick alluded, was conducted upon a rather different basis from that indicated by the banker in his conversation with Leonie.

Mr. Gunn, upon his entrance to the studio of the artist, began by expressing his regret at the issue of the breach of promise suit.

"Yes, confound it," said Mr. Weems; "it is hard, isn't it? To think that that old faded flower of a girl should be smart enough to get the better of me in such a manner!"

"The damages are heavy too," said Gunn, thoughtfully; "and I understand that she is firmly resolved to compel you to pay the money."

"That is the worst of it! The mortification was

bad enough; but five thousand dollars to pay on top of that! Why, it's simply awful."

"The amount would cover the price of a good many pictures, wouldn't it?"

"Yes; and just now the market is so overloaded with old masters, that they hardly fetch the value of the canvas they are painted on. A house-painter makes more money than an artist."

"It must be a desire for revenge that induces the lady to be so eager for the money. She is not poor."

"I guess she is. Old Cowdrick will have to give up everything, I suppose."

Mr. Gunn smiled, and looked wise. Then he said, "Mr. Weems, I'll let you into a secret if you will keep it to yourself."

"I will, certainly."

"Well, sir, I know, — I don't merely think, — I *know* that Cowdrick is going to come out of this thing with at least a quarter of a million. He'll be just as comfortable as ever."

"That is nearly incredible."

"It is the truth, at any rate; and I can prove it."

"But how about his crimes? He is tolerably certain to go to prison."

"What, Cowdrick? Cowdrick go to prison? Not a bit of it! He is too respectable. That has all been fixed in advance, unless I am misinformed."

Mr. Weems reflected in silence for a few moments. Then Mr. Gunn, rising to go, said, —

"It is none of my business, sir, of course; I only came in to give you the facts because I felt friendly to you. But if I had my choice between paying five thousand dollars and compromising with the plaintiff, I know very well what I would do, particularly if the plaintiff would rather have the man than the money. Good morning, Mr. Weems;" and Mr. Gunn withdrew.

"A quarter of a million!" said Mr. Weems to himself, as he sat alone, meditating upon the situation. "What a fool I was. I might have known that old Cowdrick would take care of himself and soon get upon his legs again. I believe that man Gunn was sent here to feel the way for a reconciliation, and I have half a notion to attempt one. I'll make a movement toward it, anyhow. I'll write a letter to Cowdrick, and if he gets out of the clutches of the law I will send it to him, and see if we can't make up the quarrel."

Then Mr. Weems went to his desk and penned the following epistle:—

"HENRY P. COWDRICK, Esq.

"DEAR SIR,—I write to you with much diffidence and with deep apprehension as to the result, concerning a matter in which my happiness is seriously involved. I need not rehearse the facts concerning my unfortunate differences with Leonie; but I wish to say that I shall never cease to regret that a mere lovers' quarrel, which should have been forgotten and forgiven a moment afterwards, should have caused, under the influence of senseless anger, a breach which, I fear, is now irreparable. For my part, reflection upon my conduct in the business makes me utterly miserable, for I cannot hide from myself, and I will not attempt to hide from you, that my affection for your daughter has lost none of its intensity because of the occurrences of which I have spoken. I love her now as fondly as I ever loved her; and though it should be ordained by fate that we shall never meet again, I shall cherish her image in my heart until my dying day, and I shall never cease to breathe earnest petitions for her happiness.

"Believe me, Yours very truly,

"JULIUS WEEMS."

"That," said Mr. Weems, "ought to bring him to terms, if he really means business."

Then Mr. Weems folded the letter, directed it, and slipped it into his pocket to await the result of Mr. Cowdrick's trial.

It would be injudicious to linger over the details of Mr. Cowdrick's trial, lest we should have a surfeit of legal proceedings. Both the prosecution and the defence were conducted with vigor and ability, and the jury, after remaining out for a very little while, found Mr. Cowdrick guilty of sundry crimes and misdemeanors of a particularly infamous character.

When the verdict had been presented, a singularly affecting scene ensued.

Amid a silence that was painful in its intensity, the prosecuting attorney, hardly able to control his emotion, rose to move that sentence be passed upon the prisoner at the bar. In doing so, he took occasion to remark that the prosecution had no desire to crush to the earth the unfortunate gentleman whom it had been compelled, in the performance of a most unpleasant duty, to arraign before the tribunal of justice. The lesson that men must not betray their trusts, and recklessly misuse the property of others, had been plainly taught by the conviction. That was the leading purpose of the prosecution; it was ample fulfilment of the demands of the law and of society, and it supplied to other men, especially to the young, a sufficiently solemn warning against indulgence in extravagance and in unwise speculation. It would be harsh — perhaps even cruel — in this instance to inflict a severe penalty, not alone because of the high social standing of the prisoner at the bar, but because it was clear enough that he did not take the money of others solely for his own benefit, but for the advancement of enterprises in which others were interested — enterprises which seemed to him likely to promote the industrial activity of the country, and to add largely to the wealth of the nation. With these remarks, he submitted the whole matter to the discretion of the Court, earnestly hoping that his Honor would find it possible to give to the prisoner an opportunity to retrieve the past by his future good conduct.

As the prosecuting attorney sat down, the courtroom was bathed in tears.

Then the leading counsel for Mr. Cowdrick arose. It was a moment or two before his feelings would permit him to command his utterance; and when, at last, he was able with a broken voice to speak, he said that he could not find language of sufficient warmth in which to express his sense of the justice, the human kindness, the frank generosity of the prosecuting attorney. These qualities, as here exhibited, did credit to his head and heart, and entitled him to the commendation of the wise and the good. The learned counsel should never for a moment believe his client to be guilty of that of which he seemed to have been found technically guilty, and he could add little to the fitting and eloquent words that had just been spoken. It had been written, "Vengeance is Mine," and it was not for an earthly tribunal to seek to inflict vengeance. His client's errors, if errors they really were, were of the head, not of the heart; and he was sure that the Court would never undertake to humiliate this excellent and worthy man, who, during a long career, had been an honored citizen of the community, by even approaching a sentence which might make him look like a felon. "I need hardly say to your Honor," continued the learned counsel, "that to impose the extreme penalty provided in this case would not only close the doors of the prison upon this estimable citizen, but would bring desolation to a happy home, would break the hearts of those who are dear to him, and would achieve no good purpose that has not already been attained." Trusting in the clemency of the Court, the learned counsel sat down, while the court-room echoed the sobs of the spectators.

The judge, wiping his eyes, and trying hard not to give way to his feelings, said, —

"Mr. Cowdrick will please rise. As you are aware, Mr. Cowdrick, I have but a single duty to perform. I must impose the sentence as it is provided by the law. I remember your social position, and your former conduct as a worthy member of society, and I have fully estimated the importance of the suggestion that your offences were perpetrated largely for the benefit of others. It gives me, therefore, great pleasure to find in the statute a limitation which enables me to inflict a penalty less severe than, otherwise, I should have been compelled to inflict. I impose upon you a fine of five hundred dollars, as provided in the statute, you to stand committed until the fine is paid."

As the judge pronounced the sentence, a great cheer went up. Mr. Cowdrick's counsel paid the fine at once, and Mr. Cowdrick, after shaking hands with the lawyers and receiving the apology of the prosecuting attorney for pushing him so hard, took his hat and walked out of the court-room a free and happy man.

Then a new jury was called to try a book-keeper,

who, because his salary was insufficient for the support of his family, had stolen three hundred dollars from his employer.

The prosecuting attorney was unable to perceive anything of a pathetic nature in the case, and when the jury promptly brought in a verdict of guilty, the judge, with a perfectly dry eye, sentenced the prisoner to incarceration at hard labor for ten years.

Although the Goddess of Justice is blindfolded, she has sometimes a very discriminating sense of the relative importance of sinners who come to her for judgment.

CHAPTER VI.

CONGRATULATIONS. — RECONCILIATION. — TRUE LOVE TRIUMPHANT. — THE WEDDING. — THE END.

ONE of the first of Mr. Cowdrick's friends who called to congratulate him upon the result of the painful ordeal to which he had been subjected was Father Tunicle.

"It must have been," said the faithful pastor, "a terrible strain upon a man of delicate sensibility to sit there, uncertain what your fate would be. I sympathize with you heartily, and rejoice that the end was not worse."

"You are very kind," said Mr. Cowdrick, smiling. "Life is full of sorrows and afflictions for all of us; and of course I cannot expect to escape bearing my share of them."

"No; and it is a comfort to reflect that these troubles are sent to us for our good. I shall expect you now to be a more efficient worker than ever at St. Cadmus's."

"I don't know," replied Mr. Cowdrick reflectively. "Possibly it might be better, all things considered, if I should not resume my official position in the church."

"But, really, you must," answered Father Tunicle. "You are still a member of the vestry, and matters will move more smoothly now, for Yetts has resigned. He was the thorn in my side."

"Where has Yetts gone?"

"I believe he has taken a pew at St. Sepulchre's, which, you know, is extremely Low Church. Poor Yetts! He has fallen very far! Do you know that the rector of St. Sepulchre's positively will not use a red altar-cloth on martyrs' days; and that he walks to church with an umbrella upon the Festival of St. Swithin, — a positive insult to the memory of the saint."

"Incredible!" exclaimed Mr. Cowdrick.

"I have it upon good authority. Such practices do much to hinder the progress of the work of evangelization."

"I should think so," said Mr. Cowdrick.

"And speaking of that work," continued Father Tunicle, "I want to obtain a little pecuniary assistance from you. I have just prepared for circulation among the depraved poor a little tract upon the sufferings of St. Blasius of Cappadocia, but I have not money enough to print it. Can you help me?"

"Certainly. How much do you want?"

"Fifty dollars are all that I ought to ask for. That sum, I think, will enable me to increase the religious fervor of the poor in my parish to a notable extent."

Mr. Cowdrick handed the money to the devoted clergyman, who thereupon withdrew.

Another early caller upon Mr. Cowdrick was an agent of the Widows' and Orphans' Life Assurance Company, in which the banker held a policy. This gentleman, representing a corporation which a week before was preparing to take legal measures to contest Mrs. Cowdrick's claim, brought with him the Company's last annual statement, and a formidable array of other documents, with an intent to persuade Mr. Cowdrick to have his life insured for an additional twenty thousand dollars.

Upon the second day after Mr. Cowdrick's release, also, the De Flukes sent to Mrs. Cowdrick an invitation to a kettle-drum, together with a note explaining that a former unfortunate recall of an invitation was due to the colossal stupidity of a servant who had since been dismissed.

This very considerate behavior on the part of the De Flukes had a favorable effect upon Mrs. Cowdrick's spirits. She brightened up in a wonderful manner, and there seemed to be every reason for believing that her load of sorrow was lifted at last.

Colonel Hoker, writing in the *Crab* of the trial and its results, explained to his readers that the verdict was rather technical than indicative of intentional wrong-doing, and he congratulated the community that one of its most enterprising and valuable citizens had succeeded in escaping from the toils of complicated financial transactions in which he had been enveloped by injudicious friends.

Colonel Hoker was disposed to criticise with some degree of severity Coroner McSorley's absurd, not to say wicked, performances with the unearthed bones; but the violence of the indignation with which he contemplated the phenomenal stupidity and the grasping avarice of the coroner, with respect to the remains in question, was greatly tempered by the consideration that Coroner McSorley's brother was sheriff of the county, with an advertising patronage estimated by good judges to amount to not less than fifty thousand dollars a year.

When Mr. Cowdrick received the note addressed to him by Mr. Weems, he replied briefly, asking the artist to call upon him at his residence; and when Mr. Weems did so, Mr. Cowdrick received him with gravity, and with some degree of coolness.

"Mr. Weems," said the banker, "I sent for you because I wished to discuss with you the matter referred to in your note My first impulse was to take no notice of the communication, for I will not conceal from you that your treatment of my daughter had embittered me against you to such an extent, that I felt as if I could never forgive you. But my child's happiness must be considered before my own feelings. It is my duty and my privilege so to consider them; and, to be frank with you, her sufferings have been so intense within the last few days, that I have felt myself willing to make almost any sacrifice in order to alleviate them."

"Miss Leonie is not ill, I trust?" asked Mr. Weems, with an admirably simulated look of alarm upon his countenance.

"Mr. Weems," said Mr. Cowdrick, seriously, "it may be injudicious for me to say so to you, because it will give you an unfair advantage at the outset; but Leonie has been deeply distressed at your treatment of her. If I were a sentimental man, I should say that her heart is breaking. She refuses food, she is continually downcast and melancholy, and in her broken sleep she babbles continually of you."

"Poor thing!" said Mr. Weems, wiping his eyes.

"Mrs. Cowdrick and I have been much distressed because of her condition; but we should have been at a loss for a remedy if your note had not suggested one."

"I have been equally unhappy myself," said Mr. Weems. "I wrote because I could find relief for my feelings in no other manner."

"Now that you are here," continued Mr. Cowdrick, "we might as well have a complete understanding. Are you prepared to make a proposition of any kind?"

"I should like to offer a suggestion, if I dared."

"You have my permission to speak freely; and I would add, in order to remove any misapprehension, that Leonie Cowdrick need not seek an alliance unless she chooses to do so, for her parents are well able to maintain her in luxury."

"Well, Mr. Cowdrick," replied Mr. Weems, "what I have to say is, that if Leonie can forgive and forget the past, it will give me the greatest happiness to renew my engagement with her, and to return to the conditions that existed before that miserable quarrel occurred. Do you think she will consent?"

"Under some pressure from me and from her mother, I think she will. For my part, I am willing to overlook what has happened, and to receive you once more into my family."

Mr. Cowdrick extended his hand, and Mr. Weems shook it warmly.

"And now, Mr. Weems," said Mr. Cowdrick, "there's another matter, of which I wish to speak. I refer to your art. Pardon me for asking you, but although I shall make some provision for Leonie, you, of course, must do something also. What is the condition of your art — in a financial sense, I mean?"

"Well, business is a little dull just at this moment."

"I thought so. The proportion of old masters in the market to the purchasing population is too great. Can't you take up something else?"

Mr. Weems reflected for a moment upon the painful lack of opportunities to rob banks with impunity and profit, and then said, —

"No; I am afraid not. I am a painter and must live by painting."

"Just so; but why not paint pictures that can be sold readily?"

"There is no money in landscapes, still-life, or figure-pieces, unless a man has genius. A painter of ordinary powers has no chance."

"But why not imitate genius, just as you imitate the old masters?"

"How do you mean?"

"Genius is apt to be eccentric. If you make a show of eccentricity, most persons will accept that as a sure token of genius. You want to be odd, novel, peculiar, altogether different from other people."

"There may be something in that."

"Paint a Venus with feet like a fishwoman, and with a cast in her eye. Paint a Moses with a moustache and spectacles. Daub off a jet-black night-scene, in which you can perceive nothing but absolute, impenetrable gloom, and label it 'A Meditation upon Darkness;' cover a canvas with blots of white paint, with nothing but the bowsprit of a ship visible, and call it 'A Misty Morning in the Harbor.' That is the way to provoke criticism and discussion, to acquire notoriety, and to find purchasers."

"It is a good idea," replied Mr. Weems. "I am much obliged to you for it; I will accept it, and act upon it."

"Would you like to see Leonie before you go?" asked Mr. Cowdrick.

"If she is willing, I should very much."

"I will speak to her about it, and prepare her for the interview," said Mr. Cowdrick, withdrawing from the room.

A moment later he returned with Leonie upon his arm. She had her handkerchief to her eyes.

"Leonie," said Mr. Cowdrick, "this is Julius. He asks you to forgive him."

Leonie lifted up her head, and the lovers looked at each other for an instant. Then she flew into his arms before a word had been spoken by either of them, and as he clasped her closely, she nestled her head upon his bosom.

Mr. Weems retained his self-possession so perfectly during this touching scene that he was conscious of the fracture of some cigars in his waistcoat pocket by the presence of Leonie's shoulder; but he bore the disaster bravely, without flinching.

Before he released his hold of her, Mrs. Cowdrick entered the room, and was so much overcome by

"Then she Flew into his Arms." Page 210.

the intensity of her emotions when she saw the lovers, that she dropped upon the sofa, and remained in a hysterical condition for at least ten minutes, despite the efforts of Mr. Cowdrick to soothe her.

When Mrs. Cowdrick's emotion had at last been brought to some extent under control, Mr. Cowdrick suggested that it might be as well to fix at once upon a day for the wedding, so that the two lovers, after all the sorrows and misunderstandings that had kept them apart, might enter the perfect bliss and the sure serenity of wedlock.

Mr. Cowdrick pressed for an early date, and although Mrs. Cowdrick betrayed new and alarming hysterical symptoms when her husband expressed the opinion that all the arrangements might be made within a week, she finally reconciled herself to the selection by Leonie of a day exactly three weeks distant.

Upon the very next morning Mrs. Cowdrick and Leonie began the work of preparation; and it is unnecessary to say that while the labor continued, both of them were in a state of nearly perfect felicity.

If earth is ever to a woman a little heaven here below, it is when she is called upon to go shopping upon a large scale with a long purse. The female mind experiences the purest joy when there are bonnets to be trimmed, fabrics to be matched, dresses to be made, underclothing to be stitched and frilled, pillow-cases and sheets to be made up, towels to be fringed and marked, furniture to be selected, crockery to be purchased, and a general fitting-out to be undertaken. Mrs. Cowdrick soon had a dozen sempstresses employed, and every day she and Leonie, in a frame of exquisite happiness, made the round of the shops, gathering huge heaps of parcels. One single touch of alloy came to mitigate the intensity of their enjoyment. The diamond merchant and the dealer in sealskin sacques, having learned from harsh experience the peril of Mrs. Cowdrick's enthusiasm for nice things, unkindly insisted upon making their contributions to Leonie's outfit upon a basis of cash in hand before delivery of the goods. But then we must not expect to have absolutely pure joy in this world.

Cards for the wedding were sent out at once to all of the friends of the bride and groom, and of Mr. and Mrs. Cowdrick. Of course, it can hardly be expected that the union of two lovers should excite very tender sympathy among disinterested persons; but it is rather melancholy to reflect that most of the individuals who received cards from the Cowdricks did not accept the compliment with unmixed satisfaction. The first thought that occurred to them upon reading the invitation was that they would be compelled to expend something for wedding presents, and many of them had a feeling, not clearly defined, but still strong, that the marriage of Cowdrick's daughter was somehow a mean kind of an attempt on Cowdrick's part to levy tribute upon them.

The presents, however, soon began to come in. Father Tunicle was heard from among the first. He sent a sweet little volume of his sermons (the lithographed discourse not being included among them). The book had been published at the cost of a few of the reverend gentleman's admirers, whose expectations of the result were rather disappointed by the sale of no more than thirty-four copies within two years. Father Tunicle sent the book to Leonie, with a touching note, requesting her especial attention to the sermon upon Auricular Confession, upon page 75. Colonel Hoker, of the *Crab*, sent a handsome silver-plated tea-set, whose value to Leonie was not in any manner decreased by the circumstance, unknown to her, that the Colonel had taken it from a former advertiser in payment for a bad debt. The De Flukes sent a pair of elegant fish-knives quite large enough to have served at a dinner where a moderate-sized whale should follow the soup, and certainly utterly useless for the dissection and distribution of any fish of smaller dimensions than a sturgeon. The Higginses, who were not in very good circumstances, and who were trying hard to save up enough money to pay for a fortnight's visit to the seaside in the summer, reluctantly sent a cake-basket, because Mr. Cowdrick had given one to Maria Higgins the year before, upon the occasion of her union with Dr. Turmeric. If Mr. Higgins had ventured, in the note he sent with the gift, to express his true feelings, the vehemence of his utterance would have made Leonie's head swim; but, happily, he controlled himself.

A perfect outrage was, however, perpetrated by Mr. John Doubleday, who had lost heavily by the failure of Mr. Cowdrick's bank. He positively had the impudence to enclose to Leonie, with his compliments, a cheque for one hundred dollars upon the aforesaid late financial institution. Mr. Cowdrick said that a man who was capable of doing a thing of that kind was not fit to live in civilized society.

Mr. Weems's artist friends all sent pictures, evidently with an intent that Weems should begin his married life with the walls of his dwelling covered with "pot-boilers," whose unsalable qualities made them as ineffective in that capacity as they were in their pretensions to be regarded as works of art. Weems felt, as he surveyed the collection, that there must have been among the brethren an organized conspiracy to unload upon him the corners of the studios.

Among the other presents received were travelling-cases, which held nothing that anybody ever wants upon a journey; cheap spoons put into a case marked with the name of a first-class silversmith, with an intent to create a wrong impression respecting the quality of the wares; and a host of trifles, most of them completely useless, and all of them accounted by the bride and groom as so much spoil collected under the duress of a custom which is idiotic when it requires anything that is ·not a genuine expression of affection or esteem.

At last, when every indignant friend had sent in a contribution, when all the dresses were made, the bonnets constructed, and the frippery and fiddle-faddle and frills arranged, the day of the wedding came. It must be described, of course. But why should an unpractised hand attempt to tell of it, when there is, within easy reach, the narrative written by the expert and dexterous fashion reporter of the *Daily Crab?* Far better would it be to transfer bodily to these pages that faithful and complete description.

(*From the " Daily Crab."*)

A WEDDING IN HIGH LIFE.

"St. Cadmus's Church, Perkiomen Square, yesterday was the scene of one of the most brilliant weddings of the season. For some weeks past the approaching event has been an absorbing topic of conversation in fashionable circles, the loveliness of the bride-elect, the popularity of the fortunate groom, and the high social standing of all the interested parties having invested the matter with more than ordinary importance. The bride was Miss Leonie Cowdrick, only daughter of the well-known ex-banker and philanthropist, Henry G. Cowdrick, Esq., and herself one of the leading belles of the *bon ton.* The groom was Julius Weems, Esq., the artist, a man whose skill as a wielder of the brush, not less than his qualities of head and heart, have made him the idol of a large circle of friends.

"The wedding ceremony was announced for half-past four in the afternoon ; and long before that hour the streets in the vicinity of St. Cadmus's were thronged with equipages belonging to the *élite* of our society. None were admitted to the church but those who were so happy as to possess cards ; the edifice, however, was densely thronged, with the exception of the pews which were reserved in the front for the immediate family and near relatives of the high contracting parties.

"The ushers, who officiated with rare delicacy and discrimination, were Messrs. Peter B. Thomas, Arthur McGinn Dabney, G. G. Parker, and Daniel O'Huff—all of them brother artists of the groom's, and men well known in cultivated circles.

"Professor Peddle presided at the organ, and previous to the arrival of the bridal party he discoursed most delicious music.

"Among the distinguished persons who graced

the occasion with their presence, we noted the following: —

"Major-Gen. Bung, Colonel Growler, Professor Boodle, Rev. Dr. Wattles, Judge Potthinkle, Captain Dingus, Major Doolittle, Hon. John Gigg, M.C., Judge Snoozer, of the Supreme Court; Miss Delilah Hopper (Minnie Myrtle), the famous authoress of 'The Bride of an Evening,' 'A Broken Heart,' etc., etc., Professor Blizzard, State Entomologist; Governor Tilby, Ex-Governor Raffles, Dr. Borer, U.S.A.; Rear-Admiral Mizzen, U.S.N.; Senator Smoot, Signor Portulacca, the Venezuelan Ambassador, General Curculio, Minister from Nicaragua; General Whisker, the railroad magnate; Colonel and Mrs. Grabeau, Dr. Hummer, Thos. G. Witt, Esq., Hon. John Grubb, Captain Mahoney, of the State Militia; Professor Smith, of the University; Galusha M. Budd, President of the Board of Trade; Hon. P. R. Bixby, Mayor of the City; and many others.

"At precisely five o'clock, Rev. Mr. Tunicle entered the church in full ecclesiastical vestments, accompanied by Rev. Dr. Pillsbury, and by Rev. John A. Stapleton, an uncle of the bride's. At this juncture the organ sounded the first notes of the Coronation March from 'Il Prophete,' and the bride entered upon the arm of her father. Following her came the groom, with Miss Lillie Whackle, the first bridesmaid, and these were succeeded by the remainder of the bridal party.

"The bride was dressed with exquisite taste, in a white satin costume, which had creamy lace in jabots down the waist and sides, mingled with pearl trimmings; while the sleeves coming only to the elbow, were made entirely of lace. The back was left quite plain, with waist and skirt in one. Upon her head she wore a dainty wreath of orange blossoms, and, of course, the usual veil.

"Among other costumes in the bridal party, we noticed a Lyons tulle, made up over satin, with flowing rosettes, and ribbons of white satin for trimming.

"Attention was directed also to a white tarletan trimmed with Breton lace and insertions, and covered with bows and loops and ends of satin ribbon.

"One of the ladies of the party wore a distinguished costume of cream-colored satin, with paniers of Pekin grenadine, with stripes of white alternating with stripes of cream-color; there was a satin corsage, plain, like a basque; and across the front-breadths of the skirt there were soft puffs of satin and grenadine.

"Mrs. Cowdrick, the mother of the bride, appeared in a regal toilette of black velvet and diamonds.

"The ceremony was read in a deeply impressive manner by Rev. Mr. Tunicle, the bride being given away, of course, by her father.

"Mrs. Cowdrick was so strongly affected by the consciousness that her daughter was being taken from her, that at the conclusion of the ceremony she displayed some slight hysterical symptoms, which for a moment threatened to create confusion. She became calmer, however, and was led out from the church by one of the ushers, weeping.

"Professor Peddle then began Mendelssohn's Wedding March, and the proud and happy groom, with his lovely wife upon his arm, turned to lead the bridal party down the aisle.

"We learn that a magnificent entertainment was given later in the day at the residence of Mr. Cowdrick, to his friends, and that the festivities were prolonged until a late hour. It is understood that the newly-married couple will spend their honeymoon at Saratoga."

The reporter was not admitted to the entertainment, and so there is upon record no description of it. But we might, if we chose, safely guess at hot rooms, so crowded that motion was nearly impossible; at absurd attempts to dance within narrow spaces; at rows of wall-flowers along the sides of the rooms; at inane attempts at conversation between guests who were strangers to each other; of groups of uncomfortable people trying to appear as if they felt very happy; of a supper-table loaded with rich viands for which well-dressed men scrambled as if they had been fasting for weeks; of ices spilled upon costly dresses, and champagne glasses emptied upon fine coats; and, finally, of departing guests in the gentlemen's dressing-rooms, saying unhandsome things to each other in sneering whispers of the man whose hospitality they had accepted.

We can imagine these things; and perhaps if we could have looked into the house at two o'clock in the morning when the last guest had said farewell, we might have heard Mr. Cowdrick say, as he threw himself weary and worn in an easy-chair, —

"Well, thank goodness, Louisa, Leonie is off of our hands at last!"

AN OLD FOGY.

"THE good old times! And the old times *were* good, my dear; better, much better, than the times that you live in. I know I am an old fogy, Nelly," said Ephraim Batterby, refilling his pipe, and looking at his granddaughter, who sat with him in front of the fire, with her head bending over her sewing; "I know I am an old fogy, and I glory in it."

"But you never will be for me, grandpa," said Nelly, glancing at him with a smile.

"Yes, my dear, I am for everybody. I am a man of the past. Everything I ever cared for and ever loved, excepting you, belongs to the years that have gone, and my affections belong to those years. I liked the people of the old time better than I do those of the new. I loved their simpler ways, the ways that I knew in my boyhood, threescore and more years ago. I am sure the world is not so good as it was then. It is smarter, perhaps; it knows more, but its wisdom vexes and disgusts me. I am not certain, my dear, that, if I had my way, I would not sweep away, at one stroke, all the so-called 'modern conveniences,' and return to the ancient methods."

"They were very slow, grandpa."

"Yes, slow; and for that I liked them. We go too fast now; but our speed, I am afraid, is hurrying us in the wrong direction. We were satisfied in the old time with what we had. It was good enough. Are men contented now? No; they are still improving and improving; still reaching out for something that will be quicker, or easier, or cheaper than the things that are. We appear to have gained much; but really we have gained nothing. We are not a bit better off now than we were; not so well off, in my opinion."

"But, grandpa, you must remember that you were young then, and perhaps looked at the world in a more hopeful way than you do now."

"Yes, I allow for that, Nelly, I allow for that; I don't deceive myself. My youth does not seem so very far off that I cannot remember it distinctly. I judge the time fairly, now in my old age, as I judge the present time, and my assured opinion is that it was superior in its ways, its life, and its people. Its people! Ah, Nelly, my dear, there were three persons in that past who alone would consecrate it to me. I am afraid there are not many women now like your mother and mine, and like my dear wife, whom you never saw. It seems to me, my child, that I would willingly live all my life over again, with its strifes and sorrows, if I could clasp again the hand of one of those angelic women, and hear a word from her sweet lips."

As the old man wiped the gathering moisture from his eyes, Nelly remained silent, choosing not to disturb the reverie into which he had fallen. Presently Ephraim rose abruptly, and said, with a smile,—

"Come, Nelly dear, I guess it is time to go to bed. I must be up very early to-morrow morning."

"At what hour do you want breakfast, grandpa?"

"Why, too soon for you, you sleepy puss. I shall breakfast by myself before you are up, or else I shall breakfast down town. I have a huge cargo of wheat in from Chicago, and I must arrange to have it shipped for Liverpool. There is one thing that remains to me from the old time, and that is some of the hard work of my youth; but even that seems a little harder than it used to. So, come now; to bed! to bed!"

While he was undressing, and long after he had crept beneath the blankets, Ephraim's thoughts wandered back and back through the spent years; and, as the happiness he had known came freshly and strongly into his mind, he felt drawn more and more towards it; until the new and old mingled together in strange but placid confusion in his brain, and he fell asleep.

When he awoke it was still dark, for the winter was just begun; but he heard — or did he only dream that he heard? — a clock in some neighboring steeple strike *six*. He knew that he must get up, for his business upon that day demanded early attention.

He sat up in bed, yawned, stretched his arms once or twice, and then, flinging the covering aside, he leaped to the floor. He fell, and hurt his arm somewhat. Strange that he should have miscalculated the distance! The bed seemed more than twice as high from the floor as it should be. It was too dark to see distinctly, so he crept to the bed with extended hands, and felt it. Yes, it was at least four feet from the floor, and, very oddly, it had long, slim posts, such as bedsteads used to have, instead of the low, carved footboard, and the high, postless headboard, which belonged to the bedstead upon which he had slept in recent years. Ephraim resolved to strike a light. He groped his way to the table, and tried to find the match-box. It was not there; he could not discover it upon the bureau either. But he found something else, which he did not recognize at first, but which a more careful examination with his fingers told him was a flint and steel. He was vexed that any one should play such a trick upon him. How could he ever succeed in lighting the gas with a flint and steel!

But he resolved to try, and he moved over

towards the gas-bracket by the bureau. It was not there! He passed his cold hand over a square yard of the wall, where the bracket used to be, but it had vanished. It actually seemed, too, as if there was no paper on the wall, for the whitewash scaled off beneath his fingers.

Perplexed and angry, Ephraim was about to replace the flint and steel upon the bureau, and to dress in the dark, when his hand encountered a candlestick. It contained a candle. He determined to try to light it. He struck the flint upon the steel at least a dozen times, in the way he remembered doing so often when he was a boy, but the sparks refused to catch the tinder. He struck again and again, until he became really warm with effort and indignation, and at last he succeeded.

It was only a poor, slim tallow candle, and Ephraim thought the light was not much better, than the darkness, it was so dim and flickering and dismal. He was conscious then that the room was chill, although his body felt so warm; and, for fear he should catch cold, he thought he would open the register, and let in some warm air. The register had disappeared! There, right before him, was a vast old-fashioned fireplace filled with wood. By what means the transformation had been effected, he could not imagine. But he was not greatly displeased.

"I always did like an open wood fire," he said, "and now I will have a roaring one."

So he touched the flame of the candle to the light kindling-wood, and in a moment it was afire.

"I will wash while it is burning up," said Ephraim.

He went to the place where he thought he should find the fixed wash-stand, with hot and cold water running from the pipes, but he was amazed to find that it had followed the strange fashion of the room, and had gone also! There was an old hand-basin, with a cracked china pitcher, standing upon a movable wash-stand, but the water in the pitcher had been turned to solid ice.

With an exclamation of impatience and indignation, Ephraim placed the pitcher between the andirons, close to the wood in the chimney-place; and he did so with smarting eyes, for the flue was cold, and volumes of smoke were pouring out into the room. In a few moments he felt that he should suffocate unless he could get some fresh air, so he resolved to open the upper sash of the window.

When he got to the window he perceived that the panes of glass were only a few inches square, and that the woodwork inclosing them was thrice thicker and heavier than it had been. He strove to pull down the upper sash, but the effort was vain; it would not move. He tried to lift the lower sash; it went up with difficulty; it seemed to weigh a hundred pounds; and, when he got it up, it would not stay. He succeeded, finally, in keeping it open by placing a chair beneath it.

When the ice in the pitcher was thawed, he finished his toilette, and then he descended the stairs. As nobody seemed to be moving in the house, he resolved to go out and get his breakfast at a restaurant. He unlocked the front door, and emerged into the street just as daylight fairly had begun.

As Ephraim descended the steps in front of his house, he had a distinct impression that something was wrong, and he was conscious of a feeling of irritation ; but it seemed to him that his mind, for some reason, did not operate with its accustomed precision ; and, while he realized the fact of a partial and very unexpected change of the conditions of his life, he found that when he tried, in a strangely feeble way, to grapple with the problem, the solution eluded him and baffled him.

The force of habit, rather than a very clearly defined purpose, led him to walk to the corner of the street, just below his dwelling, and to pause there, as usual, to await the coming of the horse-car which should carry him down town. Following a custom, too, he took from his waistcoat pocket two or three pennies (which, to his surprise, had swollen to the uncomfortable dimensions of the old copper cents), and looked around for the news-boy from whom he bought, every morning, the daily paper.

The lad, however, was not to be seen ; and Ephraim was somewhat vexed at his absence, because he was especially anxious upon that morning to observe the quotations of the Chicago and Liverpool grain markets, and to ascertain what steamers were loading at the wharves.

The horse-car was delayed much longer than he expected, and, while he waited, a man passed by, dressed oddly, Ephraim noticed, in knee-breeches and very old-fashioned coat and hat. Ephraim said to him, politely,—

"Can you tell me, sir, where I can get a morning paper in this neighborhood? The lad I buy from, commonly, is not at his post this morning."

The stranger, stopping, looked at Ephraim with a queer expression, and presently said,—

"I don't think I understand you; a *morning* paper, did you say?"

"Yes, one of the morning papers; the *Argus* or *Commercial*—any of them."

"Why, my dear sir, there is but one newspaper published in this city. It is the *Gazette*. It comes out on Saturday, and this, you know, is only Tuesday."

"Do you mean to say that we have no daily papers?" exclaimed Ephraim, somewhat angrily.

"*Daily* papers! Papers published every day! Why, sir, there is not such a newspaper in the world, and there never will be."

"Pshaw!" said Ephraim, turning his back upon the man in disgust.

The stranger smiled, and, shaking his head as if he had serious doubts of Ephraim's sanity, passed onward.

"The man is cracked," said Ephraim, looking after him. "No daily papers! The fellow has just come from the interior of Africa, or else he is an escaped lunatic. It is very queer that car does not come," and Ephraim glanced up the street anxiously. "There is not a car in sight. A fire somewhere, I suppose. Too bad that I should have lost so much time. I shall walk down."

But, as Ephraim stepped into the highway, he was surprised to find that there were no rails there. The cobblestone pavement was unbroken.

"Well, upon my word! This is the strangest thing of all. What on earth has become of the street-cars? I must go afoot, I suppose, if the distance *is* great. I am afraid I shall be too late for business, as it is."

As he walked onward at a rapid pace, and his eyes fell upon the buildings along the route, he was queerly sensible that the city had undergone a certain process of transformation. It had a familiar appearance, too. He seemed to know it in its present aspect, and yet not to know it. The way was perfectly familiar to him, and he recognized all the prominent landmarks easily, and still he had an indefinable feeling that some other city had stood where this did; that he had known this very route under other conditions, and that the later conditions were those that had passed away, while those that he now saw belonged to a much earlier period.

He felt, too, that the change, whatever it was, had brought a loss with it. The buildings that lined the street now he thought very ugly. They were old, misshapen, having pent-roofs with absurdly high gables, and the shop-windows were small, dingy, and set with small panes of glass. He had known it as a handsome street, edged with noble edifices, and offering to the gaze of the pedestrian a succession of splendid windows filled with merchandise of the most brilliant description.

But Ephraim pressed on with a determination to seek his favorite restaurant, for he began to feel very hungry. In a little while he reached the corner where the restaurant should have been, but to his vexation he saw that the building there was a coffee-house of mean appearance, in front of which swung a blurred and faded sign.

He resolved to enter, for he could get a breakfast here, at least. He pushed through the low doorway and over the sanded floor into a narrow sort of box, where a table was spread; and, as he did so, he had a hazy feeling that this, too, was something that he was familiar with.

"It must be," he said, "that my brain is producing a succession of those sensations that I have had sometimes before, which persuade the credulous that we move continually in a circle, and forever live our lives over again."

As he took his seat a waiter approached him.

"Give me a bill of fare," said Ephraim.

"Bill of fare, sir? Have no bill of fare, sir. Never have them, sir; no coffee-house has them, sir. Get you up a nice breakfast though, sir."

"What have you got?"

"Ham, sir; steak, sir; boiled egg, sir; coffee, tea, muffins. Just in from furrin countries, sir, are you?"

"Never mind where I am from," said Ephraim, testily. "Bring me a broiled steak, and egg, and some muffins and coffee, and bring them quickly."

"Yes, sir; half a minute, sir. Anything else, sir?"

"Bring me a newspaper."

"Yes, sir; here it is, sir, the very latest, sir."

Ephraim took the paper, and glanced at it. It was the *Weekly Gazette*, four days old; a little sheet of yellow-brown paper, poorly printed, containing some fragments of news, and nothing later from Europe than November 6, although the *Gazette* bore date December 19. So soon as Ephraim comprehended its worthlessness, he tossed it contemptuously upon the floor, and waited, almost sullenly, for his breakfast.

When it came in upon the tray, carried by the brisk waiter, it looked dainty and tempting enough, and the fumes that rose from it were so savory that he grew into better humor. As it was spread before him, he perceived that the waiter had given him a very coarse, two-pronged steel fork.

"Take that away," said Ephraim, tossing it to the end of the table; "I want a silver fork."

"Silver fork, sir! Bless my soul, sir! We haven't got any; never heard of such a thing, sir."

"Never heard of a silver fork, you idiot!" shouted Ephraim; "why, everybody uses them."

"No, sir; I think not, sir. I've lived with first quality people, sir, and they all use this kind. Never saw any other kind, sir; didn't know there was any. Do they have 'em in furrin parts, sir?"

"Get out!" said Ephraim, savagely. He was becoming somewhat annoyed and bewildered by the utter disappearance of so many familiar things.

But the breakfast was good, and he was hungry, so he fell to with hearty zest, and, although he found the steel fork clumsy, it did him good service. At the conclusion of the meal, Ephraim walked rapidly to his office — the office that he had occupied for nearly sixty years. As he opened the door, he expected to find his letters in the box wherein the postman thrust them twice or thrice a day. They were not there. The box itself was gone.

"Too bad! too bad!" exclaimed Ephraim. "Everything conspires to delay me to-day. I suppose I must sit here and wait for that lazy letter-carrier to come, and meantime my business must wait too."

With the intent not to lose the time altogether, Ephraim resolved to write a letter or two. He took from the drawer a sheet of rough white paper, and opened his inkstand. He could not find his favorite steel pen anywhere, and there were no other pens in the drawer, only a bundle of quills. Ephraim determined to try to use one of these. He ruined four, and lost ten minutes before he could make with his knife a pen good enough to write with; but with this he finished his letter. Then he had another hunt for an envelope, but he could find one nowhere, and nothing was to be done but to fold the sheet in the fashion that he had known in his boyhood, and to seal it with sealing-wax. He burned his fingers badly while performing the last-named operation.

Still the postman had not arrived, and Ephraim, being very anxious to mail his letter, resolved to go out and drop it into the letter-box at the corner of the street. When he reached the corner, he found that the letter-box had disappeared as so many other things had done; so he resolved to push on to the post-office, where he could leave the letter and get his morning's mail. As he approached what he had supposed was the post-office, he was dismayed to perceive that another building occupied the site. The post-office had vanished.

He turned to a man standing with a crowd which was observing him, and asked him where the post-office could be found. Obeying the direction, he sought the place and found it. Rushing to the single window, behind which a clerk stood, he asked, —

"Are there any letters for Ephraim Batterby?"

"I think not," said the clerk; "there will be no mail in till to-morrow."

"Till to-morrow!" shouted Ephraim. "What is the matter?"

"The matter! nothing at all. What's the matter with you?"

"I am expecting letters from New York and Chicago. Are both mails delayed?"

"Chicago's a place I never heard of, and the mail from New York comes in only three times a week. It came yesterday, and it will come in to-morrow."

"Three times a week!" exclaimed Ephraim; "why, it comes four or five times a day, unless I am very much mistaken."

The clerk turned to a fellow-clerk behind him and said in a low tone something at which both laughed.

"How do you suppose the mails get here four or five times a day?" asked the clerk.

"Upon the mail trains, of course," replied Ephraim, tartly; and then the clerks laughed again.

"Well, sir," said the man at the window, "we don't appear to understand each other; but it may straighten things out if I tell you that the New York mails come here upon a stage-coach, which takes twenty-four hours to make the journey, and which reaches here on Mondays, Wednesdays, and Fridays."

Ephraim was about to make an angry reply, but the clerk shut the window and made further discussion impossible. For a moment Ephraim was puzzled. He stopped to think what he should do next, and while he was standing there, he noticed a curious crowd gathering about him, a crowd which seemed to regard him with peculiar interest. And now and then a rude fellow would make facetious comments upon Ephraim's dress, at which some of the vulgar would laugh. Ephraim was somewhat bewildered, and his confusion became greater when he observed that all of the bystanders wore knee-breeches and very ugly high collars and cravats, in which their chins were completely buried. Ephraim perceived near to him a gentleman who held in his hand a newspaper. Encouraged by his friendly countenance, Ephraim said to him,—

"I am rather confused, sir, by some unexpected changes that I have found about here this morning, will you be good enough to give me a little information?"

"With pleasure, sir."

"I have missed some important letters that I looked for from New York and the West. I wish to communicate with my correspondents at once. Will you please tell me where I can find the telegraph office?"

"The telegraph office! I don't understand you, sir."

"I wish to send messages to my friends at those points."

"Well, sir, I know of no other way to send them than through the post-office here."

"Do you mean to say that there is no telegraph line from here to New York?"

"My dear sir, what do you mean by a telegraph line?"

"A telegraph line — a line of wire on which I can send messages by electricity."

"I fear something is wrong with you, sir," said the gentleman gravely. "No such thing exists. No such thing can exist."

"Nonsense!" said Ephraim, waxing indignant. "How do you suppose the afternoon papers to-day will get the quotations of the Liverpool markets of to-day? How will the brokers learn to-day the price of securities at the meeting of the London Stock Exchange this morning?"

"You are speaking very wildly, sir," said the gentleman, stepping close to Ephraim and using a low tone, while the crowd laughed. "You must be more careful, or persons will regard you as insane."

"Insane! Why? Because I tell you, what everybody knows, that we get cable news from Europe every day."

"Cable news! cable news! What does the old fool mean?" shouted the crowd.

"What do I mean!" exclaimed Ephraim, in a passion; "I mean that you are a pack of idiots for pretending to believe that there is no such thing as a telegraph, and no such thing as a telegraph cable to Europe."

The crowd sent up a shout of derisive laughter and rushed at him as if to hustle him and use him roughly. The gentleman to whom he had spoken seized him by the arm and hurried him away. When they had turned the corner, the man stopped and said to Ephraim, —

"You appear to be a sane man, although you speak so strangely. Let me warn you to be more careful in the future. If you should be taken up as a madman and consigned to a madhouse, you would endure terrible suffering, and find it very difficult to secure release."

"I *am* perfectly sane," said Ephraim, "and I cannot comprehend why you think what I have said strange. I wanted my letters, and I wished in their absence to correspond by telegraph, because I am expecting a cargo of wheat to-day, which I am to ship to Liverpool by steamer."

"By steamer! There you go again. Nobody can know what you mean by 'steamer.'"

"Steamer! Steamship! A ship that crosses the ocean by steam, without sails. You know what that is, certainly?"

"I have heard some talk about a rattle-trap invention which used steam to make a little boat paddle about on the river here; but as for crossing the ocean — well, my dear sir, that is a little too ridiculous."

"Ridiculous! Why —"

"Pardon me," said the man, "I see you are incorrigible; I must bid you good morning;" and he bowed politely and walked quickly away.

"Well, well!" said Ephraim, standing still and looking after him helplessly. "It's queer, very queer. I don't begin to understand it at all, I am half inclined to believe that the world has conspired to make game of me, or else that my poor wits really are astray. I don't feel as certain of them as a clear-headed man should."

While he spoke, the bells of the city rang out an alarm of fire with furious clangor, and in a few moments he saw, dashing past him, an old-fashioned hand-engine, pulled by a score or two of men who held a rope. The burning building was not many hundred yards distant from Ephraim, and he felt an inclination to see it. When he reached the scene, men with leathern buckets were pouring water into the engine, while other men were forcing the handles up and down, with the result that a thin stream fell upon the mass of flame.

He had an impulse to ask somebody why the steam fire-engines were not used, but every one seemed to be excited and busy, and he remembered what his friend had said to him about steamers.

So he expressed his disgust for the stupidity of these people in a few muttered ejaculations; and then, suddenly, bethought him of his business.

He resolved to go down to the wharf where he had expected to ship his cargo, and to ascertain what the situation was there.

As he came near to the place, he saw that it had changed since he last saw it, but a handsome ship lay in the dock, and men were carrying bags of grain aboard of her.

"That must be my cargo," he said; "but what on earth do they mean by loading it in that manner, and upon a sailing vessel?"

He approached the man who seemed to be superintending the work, and said, —

"Is this Ephraim Batterby's wheat?"

The man looked at him in surprise for a moment, and then, smiling, said, —

"No, sir; it is Brown and Martin's."

"When did it arrive?"

"Yesterday."

"By rail?"

"By rail! What do you mean by that?"

"I say, did it come by rail?"

"Well, old man, I haven't the least idea what you mean by 'rail,' but if you want to know, I'll tell you the grain came by canal-boat."

"From Chicago?"

"Never heard of Chicago. The wheat came from Pittsburg. What are you asking for, any way?"

"Why, I'm expecting some myself, by rail from Chicago, and I intend to ship it to Liverpool in a steamer — that is," added Ephraim, hesitatingly, "if I can find one."

"Chicago! rail! steamer! Old chap, I'm afraid you're a little weak in the top story. What do you mean by Chicago?"

"Chicago! Why, it's a city three or four hundred miles west of Pittsburg; a great centre for the western grain traffic. Certainly you must have heard of it."

"Oh, come now, old man, you're trying to guy me! I know well enough that the country is a howling wilderness, three hundred miles beyond Pittsburg. Grain market! That's good!"

"I don't know," said Ephraim, somewhat feebly. "It used to be there. And I expected a cargo of wheat from Chicago to be here this morning, by railroad."

"What kind of a railroad?"

"A railroad: iron rails, with cars propelled with steam! I expected to find an elevator here to put the grain on board of an iron vessel; to load the whole twenty thousand bushels to-day; but things have gone wrong somehow, and I don't understand precisely why!"

"Bill," said the man, turning to a young fellow, one of his assistants, near him, "trot this poor old chap up to the mayor's office, so that he'll be taken care of. He's talking to me about bringing twenty thousand bushels of wheat on a rail, and loading it in an iron vessel — an iron vessel, mind you — in one day! It's a shame for the old fellow's relations to let him wander about alone."

Before "Bill" had a chance to offer his assistance, Ephraim, alarmed, and more than ever bewildered, walked quickly away.

As he gained the street, a man of about middle age suddenly stopped in front of him, and said, —

"Good morning, Mr. Batterby."

Ephraim had gotten into such a frame of mind, that he was almost startled at the sound of his own name.

He looked hard at the stranger, but, although the features were somewhat familiar, he could not really recognize the man.

"Don't know me, Batterby? Impossible! Don't know Tony Miller!"

"Bless my soul!" exclaimed Ephraim; "Tony

Miller! so it is! Tony Miller! Not Tony Miller? Why — why — why, Miller, I thought you died thirty years ago!"

"Died! ha, ha! Not a bit of it, man. Why, it's absurd! I saw you only two or three weeks since!"

"Strange, strange!" said Ephraim, almost sadly, in his mind trying to recall some fragments of the past. "I could have sworn that you were dead!"

"No, sir; just as hearty and lively as I ever was. By the way, Mr. Batterby, what has become of Ephraim? I don't see him about any more."

"Ephraim? Ephraim Batterby? Why, who do you think I am?"

"Joshua Batterby, of course; who else? You don't seem very well to-day, I think."

"He mistakes me for my father," said Ephraim to himself. "When will all this wild, puzzling mystery end?" Then, addressing Miller, he said, "I would like to have some conversation with you, Miller; I am strangely confused and upset to-day."

"Certainly; be glad to have a chat with you. I say, suppose you come home and dine with me? I am on my way to dinner now. Will you go?"

"Gladly," replied Ephraim.

As they walked on, Miller, with intent to break the silence, said, —

"I think we shall have rain to-day, Mr. Batterby."

"Perhaps; it looks like it. What does the signal service say?"

"What does the *what* say?"

"The signal service. What are the indications?"

"I haven't the least idea what you mean, Mr. Batterby."

"Why," said Ephraim, timidly, "were you not aware that a bureau in the War Department collects information which enables it to indicate approaching conditions of the weather, and that it gives this information to the newspapers?"

"Never heard of such a thing, Mr. Batterby, and I don't believe it. Somebody has been joking with you. The only weather indications we have are in the almanacs, and they are not at all reliable."

The two walked along in silence for a time, and then Ephraim said, —

"Miller!"

"Well?"

"I am going to ask you a good many queer questions to-day, for a private purpose of my own; will you agree to answer them candidly?"

"If I can."

"And not to think me insane, or absurd, or stupid?"

"Of course I should not think so."

"Very well," said Ephraim; "and when we are done, I may explain why I asked them, and perhaps you can solve a mystery for me."

They reached the house and entered it. The first thing Miller did was to proceed to the sideboard, fill two glasses with wine from a decanter, and ask Ephraim to drink.

"Thank you," said Ephraim, "I never touch it."

Miller looked at him for a moment in amazement. He concluded that this must be one of the phases of Batterby's newly-developed queerness. So he emptied his own glass and put it down.

They entered the parlor to wait for dinner. Ephraim's eye was caught by a very pretty miniature on the wall.

"Who is that?" he asked.

"Mrs. Miller; my wife."

"Is it a photograph?"

"I don't know what a photograph is."

"Ah!" sighed Ephraim, "I remember. Let me ask you something else. Did you ever hear of a place named Chicago?"

"Never! there is no such place."

"You know nothing of railroads, or steamships, or telegraphs?"

"You are talking Greek to me."

"Did you ever hear of a telegraph cable to Europe?"

"Well, you *are* asking queer questions, sure enough. No, I never did."

"Is there, or is there not, a railway line across the continent to the Pacific?"

"What a funny kind of an idea! No, there isn't."

"Are there any such things as daily papers?"

"No, sir."

"One question more: I see you have a wood fire. Do you never burn coal?"

"Charcoal, sometimes, for some purposes."

"I mean hard coal — stone coal?"

"There is no such thing in existence, so far as I know. What are you up to, anyhow? Going to invent something?"

"I will tell you after awhile, may be," replied Ephraim; and then to himself he said, "I am beginning to catch the meaning of all this experience. How strange it is!"

A lady entered from the front door, and passed the parlor. Ephraim saw that she had on a very narrow dress, with a high waist almost beneath her armpits, that she wore upon her head an enormous and hideous green "calash" which bore some resemblance to a gig-top.

He had not seen one of those wonderful bits of head-gear for fifty years.

In a few moments the lady entered the parlor. As Mr. Miller presented Batterby to his wife, Ephraim was shocked to perceive that she seemed to have on but a single, thin, white garment, and that even this appeared to be in immediate danger of slipping downward. He thought it shockingly immodest, but he remembered the figures of women he had seen in the remote past, and thought he knew what this meant. So he gave no indication of surprise.

They went to the dining-room. Ephraim was very careful in conducting his share of the conversation. Mrs. Miller, unlike her husband, had not been forewarned. However, once, when she was lamenting the absence of fruits and vegetables from the markets in winter, Ephraim incautiously asked her why she did not use canned goods; and this opened the way to some vexatious questions. A little later, Miller began talking about the Warners, people whom Ephraim in his soul knew had been dead forty years; and Miller had mentioned that two of them were down with smallpox. Thereupon Ephraim asked if the malady was prevalent, and if Miller had been vaccinated. And thus again he got into trouble, for neither his host nor hostess knew his meaning. He was tripped up again by a reference to sewing-machines; and, finally, by remarking, innocently, when Miller observed that it had just begun to rain, that he was sorry he had not his rubbers with him.

But he would not try to explain his meaning when they pressed him. He had, indeed, an increasing tendency to taciturnity. He shrank more and more from the thought of attempting a discussion of the situation in which some wondrous mischance had placed him. As Miller waxed boisterous and lively in his talk, Ephraim was strongly impelled to complete reserve.

For he had creeping over him, gradually, a horrible feeling that these people, in whose company he was lingering, were not real people; that they were dead, and that by some awful jugglery they had been summoned forth and compelled to play over, before him, a travesty of their former lives.

He became gloomy and wretched beneath the oppression of the thoughts that crowded his brain. As the hour slipped away, his distress was made more intense by the conduct of Miller, who, warmed with wine, mingled oaths with his conversation. Ephraim felt as if that blasphemy came to him clothed with a new horror from the region of mystery beyond the grave. Finally, after Mrs. Miller had left the room, her husband's utterance became thick and harsh, and presently he slipped, drunken and helpless, beneath the table.

Ephraim sat alone at the board. The room grew darker, for the rain was now swirling without, against the window-panes. There was something ghastly and fearful in the appearance of the apartment. The outlines of the furniture, seen through the dusk, were distorted and misshapen. Ephraim felt as if he were in the presence of phantoms. He had the sensations of one who sits in a charnel-house, and knows that he is the only living thing among the dead.

His good sense half revolted against the fear that overspread him; but it seemed not strong enough to quell the tremulous terror in his soul; for that grew and grew until it filled him with a kind of panic. He had such a meaningless dread as the bravest know when they find themselves amid darkness and loneliness in a dwelling wherein, of late, have been pleasant company and merriment and laughter; wherein has been joyousness that has suddenly been quenched by utter, dismal silence.

He was seized by a sudden impulse to fly. He pushed away his chair, and glanced timorously around him. Then he trod swiftly, and with a fiercely-beating heart, to the hall-way. Grasping his hat from the table, he opened the door, and fled out into the tempest.

As he sped away through the gloomy street, now wet and slippery, and covered with pools of rain, it smote his heart with a new fear to think that even the city about him, with its high walls and impending roofs, its bricks and stones and uplifting spires, was unreal to ghastliness. But even his great dread did not forbid his mind to recall the mysteries of the day.

"I know," he said, as he rushed onward, "what

it all means. This is the Past. Some mighty hand has swept away the barrier of years, and plunged me once more into the midst of the life that I knew in my youth, long ago. And I have loved and worshipped that past. Blind and foolish man! I loved it! Ah, how I hate it now! What a miserable, miserable time it was! How poor and insufficient life seems under its conditions! How meanly men crawled about, content with their littleness and folly, and unconscious of the wisdom that lay within their reach, ignorant of the vast and wonderful possibilities that human ingenuity might compass!"

"There was nothing in that dreary past that I could love, excepting"—and Ephraim was almost ready to weep as he thought that the one longing of his soul could not be realized—"excepting those who were torn from my arms, my heart, my home, by the cruel hand of death."

The excitement, the distress, the anguish, the wild terror of the day, came back to him with accumulated force as he hurried along the footway; and when he reached his own home he was distracted, unnerved, hysterical.

With eager but uncertain fingers he pushed open the front door, and went into his sitting-room. There a fresh shock came to him, for he saw his wife in the chair she had occupied in the old time, long, long ago. She arose to greet him, and he saw that her dear face wore the kindly smile he had known so well, and that had added much to his sum of happiness in the years that were gone. He leaped to clasp her in his arms when he heard the sweet tones of her voice welcoming him ; his eyes filled with tears, and the sobs came, as he said, —

"Ah, my dearest, my dearest! have you, too, come up from the dead past to meet me? It was you alone that hallowed it to me. I loved — loved you — I —"

He felt his utterance choked, the room swam before him, there was a ringing noise in his ears, he felt himself falling ; then he lost consciousness.

He knew nothing more until he realized that there was a gentle knocking near to him, as of some one who demanded admittance at the door. He roused himself with an effort, and almost mechanically said, —

"Come in."

He heard a light step, and he opened his eyes. He was in his own bed-room, the room of the present, not of the past, and in his own bed. It was Nelly who knocked at the door; she stood beside him.

"It is time to get up, grandpa," she said.

"Wh—where am I? What has happened? Then, as his mind realized the truth, he said, "Oh, Nelly, Nelly, how I have suffered."

"How, grandpa?"

"I — I — but never mind now, my dear; I will tell you after awhile. Run down-stairs while I prepare for breakfast. But, Nelly, let me tell you not to believe what I said to you about the glories of the past; it was not true, my child, not true. I have learned better; I talked to you like a foolish old man. Thank God, my dear, that you live late in the world's history. No man is more unwise or more ungrateful than he who finds delight in playing the part of An Old Fogy."

MAJOR DUNWOODY'S LEG,

AND THE GREAT POTTAWATOMIE CLAIM.

AT Gettysburg, on the afternoon of the third day of July, 1863, Major Henry G. Dunwoody, of the 483d Regiment of Pennsylvania Volunteers, while leading his men into action, was struck by a shell from a Confederate battery. A moment later he was lying upon the ground unconscious, and beside him lay his left leg, severed from his body several inches above the knee.

When the fight was over for the day, the wounded Major was placed in an ambulance and taken to the hospital. A day or two later, the fever having left him, he lay in bed feeling tolerably comfortable. His mind not unnaturally turned to consideration of his wound. He began to think how very inconvenient it would be to have to hop about on one leg during the remainder of his life, and he couldn't help wondering where his leg was and what would be its fate. He suspected they would bury it; and the notion seemed an unpleasant one.

"I don't like the idea of being partially interred,"

he said; "and while I am alive, too. I am too young a man by half a century to have one foot in the grave."

The latter suggestion struck the Major as being rather a good joke. He resolved to remember it so that he could tell the surgeon.

The Major could hardly persuade himself, at times, as he reflected, that he had really lost his leg. He had a corn upon a certain toe which he could distinctly feel; there were strong sensations which indicated that the leg was still there, and he could hardly resist the impulse to try to lift it in such a vigorous manner as to kick off the covering of the bed. But he knew that this was absurd. While he was thinking about it he suddenly gave a little start, and a shiver ran through his nerves. He felt as if his leg had been plunged into some intensely cold liquid, and before he had quite recovered from the shock he was conscious of a faint suggestion of alcohol. Whether the perfume of the substance had actually greeted his nostrils, or the alcoholic flavor had been conveyed to his senses in some other way, he could not exactly define. He did not try very hard to solve the problem. This was only one of the many odd experiences of the first forty-eight hours, and he was too feeble to make such a vigorous mental effort as was necessary to their proper solution.

The Major recovered, and was enrolled in the Invalid Corps. During the succeeding three or four years he drew his pay, lived an easy life, and devoted much of his time to experimenting upon artificial legs of various patterns. He never succeeded in finding one that suited him exactly, and in the course of time he collected quite a curious lot of wooden and cork legs, which he kept standing about in the corners of his room at his boarding-house in Washington, and which were perpetually a source of nervous dread to the chambermaid, who lived in expectation that some day they would fly out at her and kick her downstairs.

One day the Major, while strolling along the street, passed the door of the Army Medical Museum, an institution into which has been gathered by the government a very large number of medical and surgical curiosities taken from the various battle-fields of the rebellion. It is the most horribly interesting place in the city of Washington — that is, to the ordinary lay observer. The surgeons and doctors, of course, regard its trophies with gleeful enthusiasm. To others it serves perhaps a good purpose in suggesting some distinct notion of the fearful suffering which was the price paid for the salvation of the Government, and it may perform a useful office in the future by indicating to persons who are burning with a desire for war and glory, that glory is one of the least obvious fruits of murderous strife.

It occurred to the Major to enter the building; and for half an hour he wandered about among the glass cases, studying curiously the strangely distorted fragments of the poor human body which are there preserved. As he turned the corner of one large case, he saw something that induced him to halt. A brief distance in front of him sat a woman intently engaged in drawing upon a piece of pasteboard which stood upon a small easel. It was so unexpected a sight that the Major could not resist the impulse to observe her for a moment. She seemed young and fair; a mass of bright golden hair fell upon her shoulders, and as she turned her head to look at something in one of the cases that she seemed to be sketching, the Major saw that her profile was exceedingly pretty.

He came a step or two closer, and noticed by means of a hurried glance that she had a strange figure of some kind upon the board; and then he passed on.

Just as he got close to her his artificial leg — a leg that he had received a few days before by steamer from France — suddenly launched out sideways. It encountered the foot of the easel, and the next instant Major Dunwoody lay sprawling upon the floor, with the easel across his back and the pasteboard picture lying upon his head. He recovered himself promptly, and turning to the fair artist, who stood above him with a look of mingled vexation and amusement upon her face, said, —

"I — I — really I am very sorry. It is shocking, but I assure you I couldn't help it. I am suffering from a wound, and — and" (the Major did not like to confess so openly to his dismemberment); "and in fact I had not complete control of myself."

The Major was a handsome man, and either his appearance, his pleading look, the pathetic tone of his voice, or all combined, touched the artist's heart with sympathy.

"Oh, never mind," she said, smiling, as the Major thought, more sweetly than woman ever smiled before. "No harm is done. I hope you didn't hurt yourself."

"You are very kind. No, I am not hurt; but I am greatly mortified at the trouble I have caused you. I hardly know how to express my disgust for my clumsiness."

"Pray do not distress yourself about it," said the artist, laughing; "the easel is not broken and the sketch is wholly uninjured. I should not have mourned if it had been destroyed. It is a mere study, and very incomplete."

"You are too generous," replied the Major; "but I will take good care not to disturb you again, if I can find my way out of here. Would you — would you — be — be — would you be good enough to call the janitor, or somebody, to help to get me upon my feet again? I cannot rise without — in fact, my wound is — is —"

"I shall be more than glad to assist you," said the artist, with a glance of pity in her blue eyes, "if you will take my hand."

The Major looked at the hand for a moment. It was extremely pretty; he had an impulse to kiss it, but he restrained himself. He merely clasped it in his own. The artist braced herself firmly, and the next instant the Major stood upright.

"I do not know how I can thank you for your kindness," he said, "but permit me to offer you my card. I have some influence, and if I can ever serve you in any way I shall greatly rejoice."

"Major Dunwoody! Indeed!" exclaimed the artist, as she read the name. "You are not one of the Dunwoodys of Clarion County, Pennsylvania, are you?"

"I was born there," replied the Major with not a little eagerness. He thought he saw a chance to acquire better acquaintance with this lovely and gifted woman. "Do you know any of our folks?"

"Oh, yes," said the artist, with a bright smile. "My mother came from Clarion County. She was a Hunsicker, a daughter of Hon. John Hunsicker, who represented the district in the forty-first Congress. I have often heard her speak of the Dunwoodys."

"Indeed," replied the Major. "I knew your grandfather well when I was a boy."

The conversation need not be given in detail. The artist and the Major developed at some length how a Hunsicker married a Dunwoody; how a Dunwoody eloped with a Moyer, a cousin of the Hunsickers; how a Dunwoody fought a duel with another Hunsicker over a political dispute, and shook hands afterwards; and how the loves and hates, and bargains and enterprises, and contests and schemes of the Dunwoodys and Hunsickers had filled the history of Clarion County for a quarter of a century past.

At last the Major said, —

"But you haven't given me *your* name yet."

"Pandora M'Duffy is my name. My mother, you know, married Senator M'Duffy, state senator. Poor father died many years ago, and we are now living in Washington."

"Studying art, I presume?" asked the Major, glancing at the easel.

"Yes," replied Pandora; "I am an artist."

"Is not this rather — rather a — a queer place to come to for sketches?"

"Oh, no," said Pandora, laughing; "I came here to study anatomy for a great picture I am going to paint. You see what that is?" said she, lifting the cardboard, and showing the sketch to the Major.

"That is a —.a — I should say that was a picture of — well, of the elbow of a stove-pipe. Isn't it?"

"You are not very complimentary," said Pandora. "I know it is very raw and unfinished; but it is at least a fair likeness of that human leg in the jar of alcohol over there."

"Oh, of course! So it is, so it is; astonishing likeness! How stupid I am! To be sure. The very image of it."

"Come now, I know you don't think so! You are flattering me!"

"No, indeed. It is wonderful! But — why, bless my soul, what on earth do you want a picture of such a thing as that for?"

"For my great painting," said Pandora, with a pretty little laugh. "I am preparing a picture, thirty-eight feet by twenty-seven feet, of George Washington cutting down his father's cherry-tree with his little hatchet."

"What for?"

"I expect to sell it to the Government, and to have it placed among the other historical pictures in the rotunda of the Capitol."

"But you are not going to put this leg in the picture?"

"Yes; I represent George as being barefooted, and having one trouser-leg rolled up."

"But then, I don't exactly see how — well, but George was a boy, and this is a man's leg."

"I know, but I am drawing all the figures on a heroic scale."

"Ah!" said the Major. Then he added, "But I must bid you good morning."

"I shall be very glad to have you come to see me," said Pandora.

"I assure you it will give me much pleasure to do so," answered the Major, with a feeling of exultation.

Then he bowed politely, and withdrew.

When Pandora reached home, she showed Major Dunwoody's card to her mother, and told her of the adventure at the Museum.

Mrs. M'Duffy sat upon the sofa and listened. She was a woman of distinguished appearance; of large frame, not corpulent, but rounded rather more than positive beauty seemed to require. Having the carriage of a queen, with a finely-shaped head, a strongly-defined chin, held well up, an aquiline nose, and piercing black eyes, Mrs. M'Duffy impressed the observer with a sense of power. The mother of the Gracchi might have been such a woman. If Mrs. M'Duffy had been born to a throne, she would have left her impress distinctly upon the history of nations.

Mrs. M'Duffy was familiar with the world. She was a woman who quickly comprehended possibilities. She clearly foresaw that Major Dunwoody might have an influence upon the future of Pandora, and the prospect was not pleasing to her.

"Pandora," she said, "I trust you did not ask this man to call?"

"Yes, I did, mother."

"I am sorry to hear it. I never liked *his* branch of the Dunwoodys. His father was mixed up with some very suspicious land speculations, and he died insolvent. Major Dunwoody has nothing but his pay. You must treat him with coolness when he comes."

"Why?"

"Why! Why, because it is very necessary that you should give him no encouragement of any kind. He is not a desirable match for you. Besides, you owe it to your family now to offer every opportunity to Achilles Smith. Mr. Smith worships you!"

"And I hate him," said Pandora, vigorously.

"Hate him, my child? Why, how absurd! Mr. Smith is a very charming man, and when he gets his Pottawatomie claim through Congress, he will be rich."

"He will never get it through; and I won't have him, if he does!"

"Never get it through, Pandora! Didn't General Belcher, the member for the ninety-sixth Kansas district, and his bosom friend, assure me positively that it would be approved during the present session?"

"His claim is ridiculous. Congress will never allow it."

"My dear! Pray don't be absurd! His claim is quite as reasonable as thousands of similar claims. The Pottawatomie Indians scalped him in 1862, and he very properly asks the legislature of his country to compel the savages to make reparation by surrendering two million acres of their reservation. I cannot see anything ridiculous about that. If he succeeds, he will be the largest individual land-owner in the West."

"If he succeeds!"

"But General Belcher, who is pushing his case in Congress, and who is to share the property with him, positively declares that he will succeed. The General, also, makes your acceptance of Achilles the condition of his championship of your picture. He says that Congress shall buy that picture upon the day that you marry Achilles Smith!"

"General Belcher is simply disgusting, mother. I would never think of accepting a favor from him."

"Not when his exertions can lift you and your mother out of poverty, Pandora? You talk most unreasonably."

"I mean what I say," said Pandora firmly.

"Very well, Miss, we shall see," replied Mrs. M'Duffy, rising and sweeping majestically from the room.

Major Dunwoody called upon that very evening. He called again the next evening. He called frequently upon following evenings; and although Mrs. M'Duffy treated him with coldness which bordered upon disdain, the Major's infatuation for Pandora was so strong that he forgot Mrs. M'Duffy's incivility in rejoicing over the exceeding graciousness of her daughter.

The Major was convinced that Pandora loved him, but he hesitated to take practical measures to ascertain the fact, because he could not summon up a sufficient amount of resolution to tell her the truth about the loss of his leg. He was far too honorable to deceive her respecting his misfortune until she had committed herself to him, and he was haunted by apprehension that she might reject him when she knew the actual state of the case. A catastrophe brought matters to a crisis.

One Sunday evening the Major escorted Pandora to church. During the worship the Major felt his French leg give several very strange twitches, and he could hear a clicking sound in the knee as if some of the springs were loose and moving about in an independent manner. Pandora noticed the noise too, and leaned over to ask the Major, in a whisper, if there was not a mouse running about upon the floor of the pew. The Major said he did not think there was.

Pandora whispered that it sounded rather more like machinery.

The Major faintly intimated that it might proceed from the gas meter in the cellar, or perhaps the people in the gallery were fixing something about the organ.

The Major had always rather doubted the springs in the knee-joint of the French leg. They impressed him as being far more complicated and ingenious than was necessary for simple purposes of locomotion. He was thinking about them tremulously when the sermon began. The preacher had hardly announced his text when the Major's leg suddenly flew up, kicked the bonnet upon the head of the lady in front of him over the wearer's eyes, and finally the leg fell upon the top of the back of the pew, where it kicked away vigorously. The Major, blushing crimson, grasped it and pulled it down by a severe effort. The wearer of the bonnet looked at him with indignation. Pandora seemed ready to faint.

When the Major let go his hold of the leg it bounced up again, and performed the most eccentric movements upon the back of the pew. Pandora could not suppress a faint scream; and the entire congregation stared at the miserable Major as he seized the leg and thrust it down into the pew. He held it down firmly, but the springs were strong, and they forced the toes to beat a wild tattoo upon the wooden partition in front of them.

In an agony of mortification, the Major rose, with the intention to leave the building. The sexton, who had approached him to ascertain the cause of the disturbance, gave him his arm, and the Major hopped down the aisle with his horrible leg flying out behind and before in a convulsive manner, kicking the sexton, banging pew-doors, and behaving generally in a most sensational and exciting manner.

Pandora followed her lover at a short distance. When the porch of the church was reached, the leg was still in a condition of violent agitation, and the Major, wild with shame and rage, said to the sexton,—

"Take it off! Unbuckle it! Take it off quick!"

The sexton bravely approached, fumbled about for a moment in search of the strap, and an instant later the Major's imported leg lay upon the carpet squirming about, kicking viciously, and leaping hither and thither like a wounded and desperate animal.

"Call a carriage," gasped the Major, as he leaned against the wall.

The sexton dispatched a boy for a vehicle, and when it came he placed the Major within, helped Pandora to a seat, and the party moved toward home.

For a little while neither the Major nor Pandora spoke. The situation seemed too awful for words. The silence was becoming embarrassing, when suddenly Pandora said, —

"Poor man!"

"What, are you sorry for me?" asked the Major eagerly.

"Indeed I am. How you must have suffered!"

"I thought you would hate me for subjecting you to such mortification."

"But you couldn't help it. I would be very unjust to blame you."

"And you do not dislike me because I am so crippled?"

"How could I? You are a soldier. You lost your leg honorably, did you not?"

"It was shot away at Gettysburg."

"You lost it to save my country, and you think I would not honor you for such a sacrifice?"

"Your kind words make me brave. If I might dare —"

"Such a hero as you may dare anything," she said.

"May I dare to ask if, while you honor me, you can also love me?"

"You may; and if you do, I will answer 'Yes.'"

"You are an angel!" exclaimed the Major.

They expressed their emotion in a very usual manner, which need not be described. When the carriage turned into the street upon which Pandora lived, she said, —

"Henry dear,— I may call you *Henry*, mayn't I ?— where *is* your leg ?"

"I left it squirming about in the church porch."

"No; I mean your real one, dear. The leg that was shot off."

"I haven't the least idea. Buried, I suppose."

Pandora was silent and thoughtful for a moment. Then she said, —

"Isn't it barely possible that one of those legs preserved at the Medical Museum is yours?"

"Well, I declare I never thought of that! Perhaps mine *is* there."

"The one I was sketching on the day I first met you was labelled — 'Gettysburg, July 3rd, 1863.' Maybe that was it."

"I will go around to-morrow and examine it. It would be very odd, Pandora dearest, if it should be mine. Wouldn't it?"

"Very. But I want you to make me a promise. If it should be yours, will you get it and give it to me?"

"If I can I will. But what on earth do you want it for?"

"For two reasons I want it: first, because if I am to marry you I have a legal right to all of you; and, second, because my George Washington has been standing upon one leg beside the cherry-tree for three weeks now, for the reason that I can't make a satisfactory study of his other leg."

"Pandora, I will gratify you if human energy is equal to the task. The impulses of an undying affection, not less than a fervid regard for the interests of high art, shall nerve me to the work."

"Thank you, darling!" she said.

Then, the carriage stopped at the M'Duffy front door. Pandora alighted, rang the bell, kissed her hand and disappeared, while the Major drove home in ecstasy to brood upon his unexpected happiness, and to fit himself with a Government leg that was numbered among the best in his collection.

The next morning he went around to the Medical Museum and examined Exhibit 1307 in Case 25, being the leg which Pandora had proposed to pass on to immortality by attaching a representation of it to her picture of George Washington.

The Major could not say with positiveness that the leg was his, but his impression that it belonged to him was strengthened by certain scars that seemed to be familiar, among them one which called up memories of a dog-bite obtained in a Clarion County orchard away back in the years of his boyhood.

A thought struck him. He called the janitor, and slipping a coin into his hand, he explained the case to that officer. At the Major's suggestion the janitor removed the specimen from the alcohol, and trod heavily upon the excrescence upon the toe. The Major yelled with pain. The identity of the limb was definitely ascertained.

"I will recover possession of that leg," said the Major as he left the building, "if I have to buy the entire collection!"

CHAPTER II.

GENERAL William Henry Harrison Belcher, member of Congress from the ninety-sixth Kansas district, sat in his room at his hotel one evening, with his feet upon the table, a cigar in his mouth, and a glass containing a mysterious liquid preparation beside him.

In appearance the General was a man of mark. His thick gray hair covered a noble head; his nose was large and curved in bold lines indicating strength; his face was closely shaven and rather inclined to pallor. He had eyes that seemed to pierce the person upon whom they rested, and when he used his feet to stand upon, instead of devoting them to purely ornamental purposes, as at present, his figure appeared tall and slender and comely. Those who did not know the General imagined, when they saw him in the Capitol, that he was some distinguished statesman upon whom rested the weight of a nation's business. Those who knew him, on the contrary, were aware that he was a man of no education, no skill in higher politics, and no principles worth mentioning. He had begun life as a mule-driver on the plains, but one day he contrived to obtain a contract for supplying a certain Indian agency with cattle. The Government paid him for fat steers, and he furnished the oldest and leanest cows he could find west of the Mississippi, and when they were weighed in pairs, he and his drover stood on the scale each time so as to bring the aggregate weight up to a comfortable figure. He made a small fortune at this business, and then he bought his way into the Legislature, and subsequently into Congress, his purpose being not so much to give his suffering country the benefit of his skill as a legislator, as to open for himself larger opportunities to acquire wealth at his country's expense. He had succeeded in several enterprises of the kind which had engaged his attention since he came to Washington, and now he was devoting attention to his great scheme for seizing the Pottawatomie Reservation as a matter of retributive justice to its savage owners. As he sat in his room, thinking upon the subject, he heard a knock at the door.

"Come in!" said the General.

Achilles Smith entered.

"Hello, Kill!" said the General, still keeping his feet upon the table. "Take a chair."

Mr. Smith sat down.

"What'll you have?" asked the General.

"Cocktail."

"Mix one."

Mr. Smith prepared the beverage, placed himself swiftly outside of it, elevated his feet until they rested close to those of the General, and said, —

"Well, how does the old thing work?"

"Oh, pretty well! tolerable! The Committee have promised to consider your case to-morrow, and I want you to be on hand, ready to tell your story. You've got it straight, I reckon?"

"Yes, I know it by heart."

"Let's see. Your theory is that you were scalped by a Pottawatomie Indian in 1862. Now, where is that scalp?"

"In my trunk. Between ourselves, you know, I bought it of an Indian in Laramie year before last."

"Very well. Now, what is the name of the Indian who scalped you?"

"Jumping Antelope, a chief."

"Under what circumstances?"

"I was trying to convert him by reading the Scriptures to him."

"See here, Kill, isn't that a little thin? He couldn't understand the language, you know. I'm afraid that won't wash."

"I translated it as I went along."

"S'pos'n' the Committee ask you to prove that you know the language?"

"I'll get off some gibberish, and you can assure them that you recognize it as pure Pottawatomie."

"Very well. Now, what particular part of the — the — Scriptures were you reading to him?"

"I dunno. Let's see; what are some of the books?"

"Don't ask me; I'm not very well posted. We used to have a Bible out in the Kansas Legislature, to swear members on, but they always kept a string tied around it, and after it was stolen a rumor got around that the clerk swore a whole House of Representatives in on Kidderminster's Digest of the State Laws."

"Jonah's the only book I recall very distinctly now."

"That'll do, if you can remember something in it. I connect it indistinctly with reminiscences of a whale."

"Yes. Well, I was trying to convert that Indian by reading to him about Jonah and the whale, when he rose up suddenly and began fumbling about my hair with a carving-knife."

"The Committee may go into detail. Now, why did he do this? Is the narrative calculated in any way to excite the nervous system of an untutored child of the forest?"

"No-no-no!"

"Nothing in it about depriving persons of their hair? Don't say Jonah was scalped, hey?"

"No."

"Did your assailant accompany the act with any conversation?"

"He merely remarked 'How!' and I thought I caught some rather indistinct reference to the Happy Hunting Grounds; but I'll only swear to 'How.'"

"'How!' They always say that. It indicates almost anything, from ferocious animosity to a desire to borrow plug tobacco. Then he took your hair, did he?"

"Sawed it right out, and would have murdered me if I had not fled."

"You dropped the Bible when you ran?"

"Yes, after snatching my scalp from his hand."

"Well, Kill, I think maybe that yarn'll pass. It's not first-rate, but there are three men in the Committee who want my vote for claims of theirs, and I have an idea they'll back us through thick and thin. My boy, don't call me a prophet if we don't snatch that Reservation before the session's out. It looks to me like a sure thing."

"I'd like to be as sure of something else I'm after," said Smith, rather sadly.

"What's that?"

"The M'Duffy girl."

"You shall have her, Kill, you shall have her. The old lady has promised me, positively."

"I thought so myself at first, but there is another man in the way now."

"Who is he?"

"Oh, a one-legged army man. She's taken a fancy to him, her mother tells me. He has a leg up here in the Medical Museum, and she fell in love with that first and it spread to the rest of him afterwards, gradually."

"That's original, anyhow."

"Wants to paint that preserved leg in her picture. Going to dovetail it on to Washington. If he can get the leg out of the Museum she promises to marry him."

"Well, *I'll* put a stop to *that*. I'll introduce a bill forfeiting to the Government for ever all the odd legs in the Museum. Kill, you mind what I tell you, and Pandora shall make *you* her model instead of this military ruin who is sparking her."

"I'd like to feel certain of that."

"You may; depend on me. A man with my war record needn't fear to offer himself to any — what is this fellow? Major, hey? — Well, I'll risk offending any major in the service."

"I didn't know you had any war record."

"Ain't I a General?"

"Oh, I know, but you can't throw a brick in the street without mowing down a couple of Generals — peace men from principle."

"But I have seen war, my boy! I was in the army, only as a Captain, I admit. But I smelt powder. Kill, I was distinguished for one thing:

other officers always lost their men, but I never had a fight that I didn't bring out one-third more men than I took in."

"You ought to have been promoted. Was it your war record that took you to Congress?"

"No, sir; it was brains — pure intellect — that did that. You know my district? Not a railroad in it. Not enough business to pay for the grease on the engines if there was a railroad. Of course, under such circumstances, the one thing all the people want worse than anything else is a railroad. People always want what they can't get."

"Of course."

"So as soon as I was nominated I hired four hundred men, divided them into squads, fitted them out with rods and chains and theodolites and other surveying apparatus, and started them all over the district, pretending to run lines. A squad would burst into a man's potato-patch and go to work. The owner would rush out and say, 'What in thunder you fellows a-doin' in that potato-patch?' And they'd say, 'We're surveying the route for old Belcher's railroad.' Then the man would fly into the house and tell his wife that Belcher was going to run a railroad through his property, and they'd go wild with joy. Kill, I carried that district by fifteen hundred majority over a man who under other circumstances would have beaten me out of my boots."

"That was genius, sir! nothing but pure genius."

"I think so; genius for statesmanship; not such statesmanship as they have in the played-out despotisms of Europe, but the kind that is needed in a new country."

"I say, Belcher, how would it do for you and me to go around and call on old Mrs. M'Duffy? I've a notion to go."

"I'm willing. Maybe we can settle the case of that dilapidated Major."

Mrs. M'Duffy was at home when the General and Mr. Smith called, and she received them with much cordiality.

The conversation naturally turned at an early moment to the subject of Smith's claim.

"By the way, Mr. Smith," said Mrs. M'Duffy, "your claim rests, I think you said, upon the fact that you were scalped? Your head has not that appearance."

"Oh, no! You see, madam, that in the lapse of years the wound has healed; a new scalp has gradually formed, so that now I appear to be merely bald. I have the original scalp at home in my trunk."

"How very interesting. Were you ever scalped, General?"

"No, ma'am, never. My custom has been to take scalps, not to lose them."

"The General is an old Indian fighter," observed Achilles.

"I was not aware of the fact," said Mrs. M'Duffy. "You are familiar therefore with the plains. Did you ever visit the Pottawatomie Reservation — Mr. Smith's prospective property?"

"Frequently, ma'am. It's the handsomest tract of ground east of the Rocky Mountains."

"You propose to live on it, when you get it, do you not, Mr. Smith?"

"On part of it. Half goes to the General; then I shall reserve 5000 acres for myself and dispose of the remainder to settlers. If I am successful in my suit with your daughter I shall build a house in the centre of my 5000 acres, and we will live there. We shall have plenty of elbow-room. She can paint pictures as big as all out-of-doors, and bigger."

"Pandora is *so* fond of the open country."

"Yes, madam, she can get half a dozen squaws to do her housework, so that she can have all her time to herself. I am going to arrange it so that she can shoot grizzly bears from the parlor window, if she wants to; and as for wardrobe! — well, I intend to buy all our clothes in New York, and they'll be of a kind that'll cause every woman on the old Pottawatomie Reservation to turn green with envy."

"Pandora ought to appreciate your kindness," said Mrs. M'Duffy; "but she is a strange girl, and, I fear, thinks more of her art than of the matters that commonly engage a young girl's attention."

"By the way, ma'am, how is the great picture coming on?"

"Slowly. Pandora made the handle of the hatchet more than twice as thick as the tree, and she had to alter it. A connoisseur, a friend of hers, also pointed out to her that in fore-shortening Washington's right leg she had made his foot appear to be resting upon a mountain upon the other side of the river. Corrections of this kind require time."

"She must hurry up, ma'am; she must hurry up," said the General; "I have everything fixed to obtain the consent of Congress to its purchase by the Government. I am going to press the resolution as soon as I hear that she has accepted Smith."

"You are *too* kind. Do you think it is likely to be favorably received? Mrs. Easby told me yesterday that Judge Cudderbury said that if George Washington could have foreseen Pandora's picture he would have had incorporated into the Constitution of the United States a section making it a felony to represent him as within a thousand miles of a cherry-tree. But then the judge, you know, has a daughter who professes to be an artist."

"Jealousy, ma'am! sheer jealousy. The judge knows no more about art, anyhow, than a Colorado mule knows about the sidereal system. Now, *my* opinion, Mrs. M'Duffy, is, that old Michael-what's-his-name, over there in Rome, couldn't hold a candle to your daughter in the matter of covering canvas."

As the General was speaking, the door opened, and Pandora entered. She spoke politely, but coldly, to the visitors, and after the passage of a few remarks about the condition of the weather, the General withdrew, Mrs. M'Duffy followed him to the hall to bid him adieu, and Mr. Smith remained with Pandora.

It occurred to Achilles that if Mrs. M'Duffy should happen to fail to return this would be an uncommonly good opportunity to speak of the state of his feelings. The thought pleased him, but it gave him some embarrassment.

"Miss Pandora," he said, "I am glad to hear that you are succeeding so nicely with your picture."

"Thank you; it *is* making some progress. I have been delayed by a few trifling alterations."

"Is the central figure completed yet?"

"Not quite finished. I did not feel sure about the left leg, and I shall make some studies before I paint it in."

"If you have any difficulty with that portion of the figure, why not omit it? Put in a bush, or a stone, or the trunk of a fallen tree, so as to hide the leg. Congress will accept it all the same."

"Art scorns such devices. And, besides, it would be rather too ridiculous to represent Washington standing astride of a log while he is cutting down a cherry-tree."

"True! true! That did not occur to me. What you really want is a good model. I think I could recommend one."

"I have one already, thank you."

"Indeed! A plaster of Paris one?"

"No; a real one."

"A real one?"

"The property of a friend of mine; a gentleman."

"On or off?"

"Off."

"Humph! That seems to me — a — a — rather a queer offering to a lady."

"Do you think so?"

"I am a plain man, not used to flattering women, but if I wished to express my regard for a lady I would offer her my heart instead of my leg."

"It would be dreadful if the lady happened not to want any portion of you, wouldn't it?"

"Yes; but suppose I should offer her the Pottawatomie Reservation besides, do you think she would refuse?"

"You had better undertake the investigation yourself. How can I know?"

"I *will* undertake it now. I offer my heart to *you!* I offer the Reservation also. I love you, Pandora. Oh, how I love you! Will you be my wife?"

"Mr. Smith, it is impossible."

"No, not impossible, Pandora. Not impossible. Do not say that; it will kill me. Listen! Have you ever dreamed of a home upon the wide and boundless prairie? A sweet little home, two stories and an attic, painted white with green shutters, where you can see eighteen miles in a straight line, where two hundred acres in potatoes lie beneath your very window, and where you can hunt the bounding buffalo and the prairie-hen without going off the estate; and where copper-colored servant girls can be had for two dollars a month and found? Have you ever dreamed of such a home?"

"Never."

"It is to it I would bear you as my bride. Come with me! Be mine! I cannot offer you the enervating luxuries of the depraved and decaying East, but together we can feast upon jerked beef and buffalo tongues; together we can drink draughts from the Artesian well in the cellar; together we will sit beneath the tree by the front door, the only one within twenty-seven miles, and together we can watch the dog chasing the jackass-rabbits across the sage brush. Be mine, and I will stock the pantry with rations from the nearest Indian agency, where I have a friend; I will buy you a suave and gentle mule for you to exercise yourself on, and you may have canvas enough to paint General Washingtons and Lord Cornwallises as high as church steeples, and I will guarantee that Congress shall bid them in as fast as you turn them out. Will you, Pandora? Do you like the promise? Oh, say that you love me!"

"Mr. Smith, I cannot. I am very sorry, but to tell the truth plainly, I am engaged to another gentleman."

"To Dunwoody?"

"I did not mention his name, sir."

"But I know him! A one-legged Major! And you refuse me for him?"

"I refuse you; that is enough."

"Oh, very well, Miss M'Duffy. I understand you. I will bid you a very good evening. I hope you will not have occasion to regret your decision."

"Certainly I shall not! Good evening, sir!"

As Achilles passed out through the hall he encountered Major Dunwoody, who was just placing his hat upon the rack. Achilles looked back at him for a second, scowling with rage and mortification, and then as he rushed into the open air, he said to himself,—

"Never mind, you hopping, mud-headed, military humbug. I'll settle *your* case before you're many days older."

And then Mr. Smith went home to bed.

Pandora greeted the Major with a joyful smile.

"Darling," said the Major, "who was that person I passed in the hall as I came in?"

"That was Achilles Smith, the man of whom I told you. He proposed to me a few moments before you came in."

"He did, did he?" exclaimed the Major savagely. "I wish I had known it. I would have kicked him down the steps."

"But how could you, dearest, with only one leg?"

"True!" said the Major. "But I could have thrashed him with my cane. So he wants to marry you, does he?"

"Yes, and mother thinks I ought to accept him."

"And you have firmly made up your mind to marry me?" asked the Major, fondly.

"Yes, dear," said Pandora, with a roguish smile, "but only when you have succeeded in getting for me your disconnected leg. You will try to get it for me soon, Henry, won't you?"

"I am trying now, my sweet. Colonel Dabney, of the Maine delegation, has already introduced to the House of Representatives a bill appropriating my leg to me."

"How splendid!"

"And he says it will pass promptly, so that I can obtain the leg within less than two months. We'll be married right off then, won't we?"

"At once. But I'm afraid, Henry, Mr. Smith and General Belcher will oppose Colonel Dabney's bill if they hear of it."

"I'll brain both of them if they do," said the Major. "No, I won't brain Smith; he has no brains. And now, Pandora, darling, let us talk of something else. Are you sure, my dearest, that you love me *very*, very, *very* much?"

"Oh, Henry! ten thousand, thousand times more than I can ever tell you. I—"

A person passing the parlor door at this juncture might have heard a sharp sound resembling somewhat that made by the tearing of a piece of muslin. The conversation need not be quoted at greater length. It appeared to give the most intense pleasure to the Major and Pandora, but talk of that kind is usually rather dreary for outside parties; so we will lower the curtain here.

CHAPTER III.

ABOUT a week later, Colonel Dabney reported, with a favorable recommendation to the House, from the Committee on Public Property, "An Act restoring a certain amputated limb in the Medical Museum to Major Henry G. Dunwoody." The Act specified the leg contained in Exhibit 1307, Case 25, as the property to be restored.

When the bill came up for discussion, General Belcher moved to lay it upon the table. Defeated. Then he moved to amend it with a provision that the bone of the leg should be withdrawn and retained in the Museum. Rejected. Then he offered a resolution referring the whole matter to a committee of inquiry, which should be directed to sit for two years, and to take testimony as to what had been the practice of governments in the matter of surrendering legs blown off in battle, from the time of Sennacherib down to the battle of Sedan, including evidence respecting the custom in Persia, Greece, Egypt, Rome, Carthage, Palestine, and modern Europe. After a spirited debate the resolution was lost. But the General was not discouraged. He presented another resolution, that a special committee be directed to inquire whether the person mentioned in this bill was the same Major Dunwoody who, in a fit of alcoholic frenzy, in Clarion County, Pennsylvania, in 1866, treed his aged grandfather one rainy night, and compelled that venerable and rheumatic person to roost upon a lofty branch until morning. Voted down: Yeas 304; Nays 1 (General Belcher).

The bill finally passed to a third reading, and was adopted. When it had received the approval of the Senate and the President, Major Dunwoody drove round to the Museum in high glee with Pandora. He carried in his pocket an empty pillow-case, in which he proposed to take home with him the long-lost fragment of himself. When he found the janitor and presented his credentials, that official was exceedingly polite, and at once led the way to the place where the treasure was kept.

While he was unlocking the case, Pandora could hardly repress her feelings of joy. Leaning upon her lover's arm, and watching the janitor, she exclaimed, —

"Isn't it elegant, dear? I can hardly realize that we are really going to get it! Mother will be so glad when George Washington has his other leg on."

"I wish I had *my* other one on," said the Major, pleasantly.

"So do I. It's too bad! But you can stand it up on the table and look at it now as much as you want to, can't you, darling?"

The janitor lifted down the huge jar containing the limb, and took it out of the spirits.

"I feel," said the Major, as he unfolded his pillow-case, "as if I was in a cemetery, disinterring one of my near relations."

"So beautiful! Isn't it?" said Pandora.

The Major suddenly scrutinized the leg closely.

"Why, how — how's this? I don't exactly understand — let's see, janitor, this is Exhibit 1307? Yes. Case 25? Yes, Case 25; so it is. Why, Thunder and Mars! (excuse my agitation, Pandora,) there must be something wrong about this!"

"Wrong, Henry? How?"

"Guess not, sir," said the janitor. "This is what the bill calls for."

"But it can't be, you know. I lost my left leg, and this one you had in the jar here is a right leg. I couldn't have had two right legs, Pandora, of course!"

"I do not know, dear. Some persons have peculiarities of formation which —"

"Oh, well, now, be reasonable. I am absolutely certain that my leg was a left leg in every particular. You see, Pandora, this is a matter about which I may fairly be considered an authority."

"Yes, Henry, but — but maybe being in the alcohol so long may have changed it."

"Impossible. Quite impossible, Pandora. The annals of medical science, from Esculapius down, contain no record of such a thing. The leg is not mine."

"But you might as well take it, dearest, mightn't you, because my George Washington ought to be finished as quickly as possible?"

"You don't want to put two right legs on him, too, do you?"

"I don't know, Henry, I might. People won't look at his toes; and if they did, they would regard the arrangement as one of the eccentricities of genius, perhaps."

"Let us look about," said the Major. "Perhaps my leg is in one of these other cases. Why, here it is! Sure enough! In Case 1236, Exhibit 11. That is mine. You'll let me have it, Mr. Janitor, of course?"

"Can't do it, sir; I have to follow the Act of Congress carefully. I daren't go outside of it."

"Well, this is too bad!" exclaimed the Major. "You positively won't give it to me?"

"No, sir; I won't."

"Well, then, Pandora, there is nothing to do but to wait. I'll get Colonel Dabney to put another bill through at once. Let me get the numbers: Exhibit 11, Case 1236."

Then, taking Pandora upon his arm, the Major hobbled to his carriage and drove straight to the Capitol.

About three weeks later another bill passed the House without opposition, General Belcher being absent in New York upon a Committee of Inquiry. While the measure was pending in the Senate, Achilles Smith, one morning, at an early hour, entered a rear door of the Museum with a key which he had obtained by bribing the charwoman, and proceeding to Case 1236, he removed the leg from the jar No. 11, and put it in another jar in another case, replacing it with the leg that had been in the latter jar.

He went down-stairs chuckling. "You mutilated outcast, you," he said, addressing the Major in imagination; "we'll see who'll beat at this game!"

When the Act had been signed by the President, the Major drove with Pandora to the Museum a second time. Upon reaching Case 1236 he was for a moment stricken dumb with amazement. Presently he said, —

"Why, Pandora, my dear, do you see? It's the leg of a colored man!"

"Ye—e—es, it seems to be, Henry. But perhaps mortification or something has set in."

"It is very mysterious. I can't account for it."

"One of your legs was not colored, was it, my love?"

"Oh, no, of course not!"

"Perhaps the janitor here has tarred it over, to preserve it better?"

"No, ma'am; that's not allowed in this institution."

"You'll take it anyhow; won't you, Henry?"

"Oh, my dear, be reasonable. Take the leg of a negro for mine!"

"Well, but, Henry, I can paint it white in my picture."

"Yes; but, Pandora, you know we won't care to have particles of fractured Africans scattered about our house. We can have no cherished memories associated with a leg like this."

"I suppose not; but it seems rather hard that my Washington should have to stand upon that one leg at least a month longer."

"He won't mind it. He was heroic. He would have stood upon a solitary leg for centuries rather than have robbed another man of his members."

Pandora sighed deeply, and made up her mind to try to be resigned; and so they went downstairs, and drove away to state the case to Colonel Dabney.

The Colonel, after hearing the story, distinctly affirmed the opinion that there had been foul play. The Major jumped at the suggestion, and told him of General Belcher and Achilles Smith, and their designs respecting Pandora.

"Never mind; I will defeat their plans," said the Colonel. "You shall have the leg next time, if it is still in existence, no matter who meddles with it."

The next Act reported by Colonel Dabney provided that Major Henry G. Dunwoody should have authority to take possession of his leg wherever it conld be found, in any institution under control of the Government.

General Belcher made a long and eloquent speech in opposition to the bill.

He referred to the heroes of the past. Who ever heard of Epaminondas prowling about in search of a leg lost in honorable warfare? Did Leonidas return from Thermopylæ to seek the aid of the national legislature in an effort to recover members of his body that had been hacked off? Hannibal was fairly torn to pieces, but he would have scorned to go fishing in alcohol jars for them. Cæsar, Alexander, Wallenstein, Wellington, General Jackson, were all mighty warriors, but he had yet to learn that they ever stooped to begging their respective governments for mangled remains that had been preserved for the instruction of medical men and the alleviation of the sufferings of the human race. No, it was reserved for this obscure American militiaman, who was gravely suspected of fiendish barbarity to an aged and infirm grandsire, and who had been charged with hiding behind a baggage-wagon at Gettysburg, to begin this ghoulish practice of grasping for legs that had been solemnly dedicated to the uses of our common country.

He would direct attention to the remarkable and mysterious circumstances surrounding this case. It was admitted even by the friends of Major Dunwoody that he had *one* leg. Two other legs had been awarded him by separate Acts of Congress. That made three. He had in his hand a receipt for two artificial legs supplied to Major Dunwoody by the Government, making five; and he was credibly informed that the Major had recently appeared at a church in the capital wearing a French leg, with which he performed some extraordinary, not to say scandalous, feats during the service. Thus there was positive evidence that this person had already in his possession six legs, and now he was demanding from Congress permission to take a seventh. He appealed to the House, was it reasonable that one man should be allowed to have seven legs? Would it look well for this House to announce to the country that it was willing to rifle the Medical Museum in order to confer an additional leg upon a man who was the owner of six others? He could understand such legislation if men were constructed like centipedes, but it seemed to him more than monstrous, positively iniquitous, indeed, to vote away the pathetic and instructive remnants of our glorious heroes for the purpose of furthering the insidious, perhaps treasonable, designs of a man who had enough legs of various kinds already to make three ordinary men comfortable.

When the General concluded his remarks, Colonel Dabney replied, and stated the facts of the case plainly and forcibly. The bill was passed by a handsome majority.

CHAPTER IV.

UPON the very same day, General Belcher's Act indemnifying Achilles Smith for the loss of his scalp by removing the Pottawatomie Indians from their reservation, was squeezed through the House by a majority of two votes. The bill provided for the immediate withdrawal of the Indians from their reservation in the Indian Territory, and the location of the tribe upon another reservation in Colorado, in a part of the country which is absolutely a desert, without water or shrubbery, and wholly unfit for the residence of any animal of a higher grade than a rattlesnake.

By some means the information of the action of the House was conveyed to the Pottawatomie chiefs, and they expressed to their agent their disgust in very strong language. The agent was scared, and he sent to Fort Gibson for a company of cavalry to protect him. The commander could spare but ten men. When the Indians discovered the approach of the soldiers they imagined that a force was coming to drive them from their homes, and accordingly they attacked the squad, killed all but one man, and then the entire tribe went upon the warpath.

The Government took instant action. The Indians numbered about one thousand warriors. The force sent to crush them included not more than two hundred cavalrymen. The Indians were mounted upon fleet and hardy ponies, which could endure an incredible amount of fatigue and live upon grass. The cavalrymen bestrode horses which had performed service in New York omnibuses and upon St. Louis horse-cars, and which could hardly be driven faster than six miles an hour under stress. The Indians were armed with telescope rifles, breech-loading, and warranted to kill at three-quarters of a mile. These had been furnished gratuitously in time of peace by a beneficent Government. The soldiers were armed with short-range carbines, and with sabres which were about as useful in fighting savages who never came within gun-shot as a fishing-rod would have been. The Indians carried upon their ponies what food they wanted. The military force was encumbered by ambulances and several wagons carrying camp equipage. In a fight at close quarters the soldiers could have beaten their adversaries easily. In a race, which permitted no other fighting than occasional skirmishing, all the chances were on the side of the Indians; and a race was what the combatants were in for.

Just before the expedition was ready to start, General Belcher, by bringing some influence indirectly to bear, succeeded in having Major Dunwoody detailed to accompany it in command of the Commissary Department. The Major was wild with vexation and disgust.

"Pandora, darling," he said, "you know that I was to get my leg to-morrow, and that we were to be married within the month?"

"Well! Won't we? Is anything wrong?"

"Wrong! Why, my dear, I have just received from the War Department orders to accompany the expedition against the Pottawatomies. I start to-morrow for Fort Gibson."

"How can you ride, with only one leg?"

"I am to command the Commissary Department. I shall have to ride in an ambulance. This is the fault of that accursed Smith. Why didn't he and Belcher let the Indians alone?"

"And we can't be married, then, until you return?"

"I don't see how. Isn't it outrageous? I have the worst luck of any man in the army."

Pandora looked as if she were going to cry.

"And your leg? Won't you get that until you come back?"

"Yes, dear, I will take it out of the Museum this evening, and you can amuse yourself throwing it upon the canvas while I am gone."

"Oh, that will be so nice!"

"So nice that I am gone?"

"Oh, Henry! How could you think I meant that?"

"I didn't; I was only jesting. And you will think of me sometimes?"

"Yes, oh yes; every moment of the day."

"And you love me very much?"

"Indeed, indeed, I do!"

"My darling!"

"My dearest!"

Probably the curtain might as well drop again at this point.

The expedition started from Fort Gibson. It marched straight across the Indian territory to the Pottawatomie Reservation. The savages had moved off, about a day's march ahead of the soldiers, toward the northwest. The military pressed forward; the Indians kept always just a little in advance. The two forces crossed into Kansas. The troops pressed their omnibus horses a little harder, and came within sight of the Indian rear-guard. Then the savages spurred up and increased the interval between them and the pursuers.

The Pottawatomies headed for Colorado, and crossed the line in a few days, with the soldiers the usual distance behind. Just after passing the Colorado border, the Colonel commanding resolved to steal a march upon the foe. One night, instead of going into camp, he pressed on until twelve o'clock, and then halted upon the bank of the Arkansas River.

Four omnibus horses succumbed under the strain, and ere morning dawned some Pottawatomies crept into the camp and stole six mules.

The most degraded Indian was never known to steal a New York omnibus horse, even in the dark.

The next day the four dismounted troopers were placed in an ambulance, and the pursuit began again. The Indians fled up through Colorado into Wyoming Territory, and the Colonel commanding pushed after them, going faster and faster every day. By the time he reached Fort Russel, just over the edge of the Wyoming line, the route of his march was marked with a succession of omnibus and car horses in various stages of decay. At the Fort he obtained fresh horses, and sacrificing the baggage wagons, keeping only the ambulances, he pressed on.

On the 27th of August his scouts discovered the Indians in camp in a valley a few miles ahead. The Colonel resolved upon a surprise. When everything was arranged the troops charged down upon the village with a wild hurrah. Not an Indian could be seen. The soldiers, however, burned the lodges and withdrew. Upon their return they found that in their absence the Indians had stampeded their mules and all their ambulances but one, which Major Dunwoody had saved by hard driving.

The chase was resumed with greater heat than ever. So far there had not been a chance for anything like a fight. In fact, not a dozen savages had been seen.

Within a week or two Wyoming was traversed and Montana Territory reached. There, just beyond the Crow Indian Reservation, the first Pottawatomie of the campaign was slain. He sneaked into the camp one night, and while cutting loose one of Major Dunwoody's mules, the mule kicked him upon the head and killed him.

On the 6th of October the soldiers had marched for thirty-six hours without rest, and it was believed that they would at last strike a telling blow upon the savages. Everything was ready for a fight, and the troops were full of eagerness for the fray. While they were halting for water upon a small creek, a friendly Gros Ventre Indian came in with the information that the fugitive Pottawatomies had crossed the British line and were now safe from pursuit within the dominions of Her Majesty.

The Colonel and his officers and men fairly tore the English language into shreds in their efforts to express with the necessary emphasis their appreciation of the facts of the situation.

The "war" cost the Government a little less than a million and a half dollars, omnibus horses included; and it was estimated by well-informed persons that the flying Indians, while upon the route, destroyed private property to the amount of half a million more, besides killing and scalping a party of eighteen emigrants which was passing through Wyoming.

It seemed like rather a large price to pay for Mr. Achilles Smith's scalp.

Some time during the month of September, while the chase was in progress, Achilles called at the house of Mrs. M'Duffy in Washington and asked for Pandora. He said, —

"Miss M'Duffy, I come upon a somewhat painful errand, but I have a duty devolving upon me, and I must perform it."

"No bad news from Major Dunwoody, I hope, Mr. Smith?"

"I am sorry to say there is."

Pandora's eyes filled with tears. Her face became pale.

"What is it?" she asked.

"I have here a dispatch to the Secretary of War, saying that in a fight with the Indians, on last Wednesday week, Major Dunwoody—"

"Not killed! Oh, please don't say he was slain! I can't bear it."

"No, not killed. Major Dunwoody has lost his other leg and his right arm."

"How terrible!" screamed Pandora; then she wept bitterly.

"Terrible, indeed!" replied Smith in a sympathetic tone. "But you know this is the fortune of war. This it is to be a soldier."

"Poor Henry! How he must have suffered! Do you know how he is? What are the chances of recovery?"

"The dispatch says he is doing very well. But of course he will be a mere wreck."

"It is dreadful, too dreadful!"

"Perfectly helpless, too. A mere burden upon those who will have to take care of him."

"Not if they love him!"

"But surely you — you do not intend to cling to such a — a — such a disintegrated ruin as he?"

"I shall be true to him unto death."

"I had hoped," said Achilles sadly, "that now that Dunwoody is reduced to about one half his original dimensions, I might hope to have you consider my claims."

"Never! It can never be!"

"Because I am about moving out on the Pottawatomie Reservation, and with you as my bride I could make it a little paradise here below. If you will take me, the Reservation is yours in fee-simple."

"I scorn the offer, sir!"

"You scorn it, do you? Scorn the most splendid tract of land in the Mississippi Valley for the sake of marrying half of a man, whom you'll have to carry to church in a market basket and to feed with a spoon!"

"Yes, sir. I scorn it and you. For to you and your wicked schemes against the unoffending Indians, this awful, this dreadful suffering of Major Dunwoody is due. I hate you! Yes, I hate you! Leave the house this instant, sir!"

Smith withdrew, and as he closed the door Pandora fell upon the sofa and cried as if her poor little heart would break.

Enter Mrs. M'Duffy.

"Pandora, my child, what is the matter?"

"Didn't that horrid Smith tell you?"

"What horrid Smith? I don't know any such person. If you mean Mr. Achilles Smith, why, he didn't tell me anything. I have not seen him."

"Poor Major Dunwoody has had his arm shot off."

"What! Not another limb lost! Why, the man is falling apart in sections."

"And that's not the worst of it."

"Not the worst? Why, my child, what do you mean?"

"His other leg has been amputated."

"Humph! Well, that's agreeable news. No legs and only one arm. Pity they didn't amputate his head at once. I suppose, of course, you will break your engagement?"

"Oh, mother! How can you be so unkind?"

"Pandora M'Duffy, you must be insane. Marry a man with only one limb. How is he going to waddle around? Do you intend to carry him under your arm, in a bundle?"

"He will go on wheels, of course," said Pandora with brimming eyes.

"On wheels! A Hunsicker and a M'Duffy married to a man on wheels, and who has to slide on the banister when he wants to come downstairs! Why don't you accept Mr. Smith at once? He is intact, I believe, with the exception of his scalp. This family seems to be haunted by men who are more or less in piecemeal."

"I would rather die than marry Smith."

"You might do it for your mother's sake, so as to be near to her."

"Near to her? What do you mean?"

"Why, I came in to tell you, my child, that I have accepted General Belcher's hand. I shall marry him, and we shall probably spend our summers at his prospective country seat upon the Pottawatomie Reservation."

"General Belcher!" exclaimed Pandora in disgust; "I never thought, mother, it would come to *that!*"

Then Pandora swept out of the room, with her handkerchief to her eyes, leaving the majestic Mrs. M'Duffy in a condition of some uncertainty as to her daughter's theory respecting the degree of humiliation which had been reached in her contract with the General.

"But I know he is rich, and that he has a promise of an appointment as Minister to Peru, where he expects to speculate in bark," said Mrs. M'Duffy to herself.

The Secretary of the Interior Department at that period was an especially capable officer. He obtained by some means a clue to the secret of the movement against the Pottawatomie Reservation, and he followed it industriously by means of his agents. Late in the month of October he had probed the matter to the bottom, and he gave it to the newspapers.

The entire conspiracy of General Belcher and Achilles Smith was exposed, and an indignant nation discovered that the costly struggle with the Pottawatomies had not even so slight a basis of justice on the part of the Government as a real injury done to Achilles Smith. It was ascertained that Smith had not been scalped at all. He had merely had his hair pulled at the Pottawatomie agency by a muscular squaw whom he was trying to cheat out of her fair allowance of rations.

It became clear that a Congressional investigation would be ordered before the year was out, and Achilles Smith fled. General Belcher's conduct excited so much indignation at Kansas, that the politicians, following the popular lead, turned on him. He was arrested and tried upon a charge of bribery, and was committed. When on his way to prison he knocked down his custodian, took the first horse he came to, and started due South. It is supposed that he went to Mexico. The feeling in Kansas is that the unhappy land of the Montezumas has yet to experience her bitterest woes. It will be a charming country to emigrate from when General Belcher begins to feel at home.

Early in November Major Dunwoody obtained release from his duties and came to Washington. He had not warned Pandora; he wished to surprise her. When he called he withheld his name from the servant. Pandora entered the room slowly. When she saw her lover she gave a little scream of joy and flew towards him. Before reaching him a thought struck her. She paused and seemed astonished.

"What's the matter, darling? Aren't you glad to see me?"

"Yes, but what — what — why — Henry dear, how is it you have your leg with you?"

"I always keep it by me, sweet. It is so convenient to have it along. You have the other one, you know."

"But, Henry, you appear to have both arms, too."

"I brought them to hug you with, you angel, you."

She flew into them, and after a brief moment expended in exercising their lips, Pandora looked up into the Major's face and said,—

"You know, dear, I heard that you had lost your other leg and one of your arms. I cried about it for a month."

"Who gave you that information?"

"That scandalous story-teller, Achilles Smith."

"Smith, hey! Is he still around? That young man is actually suffering for somebody to macerate him."

"And you're not hurt a bit, are you, deary?"

"I am a little dyspeptic from too regular dieting upon salt pork so tough that it creaked when I swallowed it; but that's all."

"Oh, Henry, you don't know how glad I am!"

More osculatory exercise at this juncture; but we will not stop to consider it, satisfactory as it appeared to be.

"And now, my love," said the Major, as they sat together on the sofa, the Major's right arm encircling Pandora's waist, "tell me about everything."

"Well, let me see. First of all — you know, mother?"

"Yes."

"Well, she is going to marry Colonel Dabney."

"You don't say so?"

"Yes; she *was* engaged to General Belcher, but —"

"Not old Belcher of Kansas?"

"Yes; but he proved a rascal, so she discarded

him, and now she is engaged to Colonel Dabney. Splendid, isn't it?"

"Perfectly splendid. By the way, have you copied my off leg yet?"

"Oh, yes; long ago."

"Then your picture is done?"

"Yes, Henry dear, but —"

"What! Isn't it satisfactory, after all?"

"It is to me, darling, but Colonel Dabney says Congress will never accept it."

"Why not?"

"He seemed embarrassed when I asked him the reason, and he turned the subject."

"Absolutely hopeless, is it?"

"Colonel Dabney says so."

"What will you do with it?"

"I don't know, dear; what do you think?"

"Couldn't you alter it into something else?"

"I thought of that. It occurred to me that maybe I might turn it into the Execution of Mary Queen of Scots and get the Canadian Government to buy it."

"Not a bad idea."

"Paint in different clothes, you know, on Washington, and fix up the tree somehow into Mary Queen of Scots. I think the hatchet will do as it is — do for the executioner's axe, you know."

"I see. It's a good notion."

"Mother said she thought I might make it a

battle between a Crusader and a Saracen, but the tree is in the wrong position for a person supposed to be fighting."

"Won't do at all, of course."

"When General Belcher was here he said he believed that by painting the grass red so as to represent fire, and making a mast with rigging out of the tree, it might pass for the Boy who stood on the Burning Deck — Casabianca. But the Canadian Government would not care particularly about the Boy who stood on the Burning Deck, would they, Henry?"

"I have a dim idea that they wouldn't."

"I think I'll stick to Mary Queen of Scots."

"And now about our wedding?"

"I'm ready."

"Name the day."

"Will next Thursday do?"

"Admirable. So, next Thursday you will be my darling wife."

"And you will be my sweet, splendid husband."

"Pandora!"

"Henry!"

Another fall of the curtain appears to be necessary just here. We will ring it down. If it could have been raised again a glimpse might have been caught of a pretty room in which sat a lovely and smiling woman by the side of a table, sewing. Close to her sat a handsome young soldier, with one leg upon the floor. His other leg bobbed about in a huge jar that rested in a corner. Pandora M'Duffy had been transformed into Mrs. Major Henry G. Dunwoody, and she was happy.

"JINNIE."

A STORY OF A CHILD.

"JINNIE! Vir-r-rginia-a-a! You 'Jin'! If you're not here in a minute, I'll whip you within an inch of your life!"

It was the shrill voice of Mrs. Tyke. Down from some mysterious part of the recesses of the house it came with the force and precision of a rifle-ball, through the narrow hall and open door to the ears of Jinnie, who was scrubbing the front steps.

Why Mrs. Tyke desired that the steps and the pavement should be scrubbed upon that cold and dismal December morning cannot be imagined. Probably she herself could not have given a reason for it if she had been asked. The bricks looked very clean and wholesome before the work began, and the marble steps were almost painfully white. Now, the pavement was covered with a film of ice upon which pedestrians slipped and were provoked to anger, and the steps were positively so icy as to be unfit for use.

The voice of Mrs. Tyke gave fresh impetus to the arm of the child, who was just giving a few finishing wipes to the uppermost step. She was a little child, surely not more than eight years of age. As she knelt upon the marble, rather painful prominence was given to a pair of shoes which might once have been the property of Mrs. Tyke herself, but which were now worn, as forlorn and riddled wrecks, upon feet which were stockingless. The thin little legs above the leather ruins were blue with cold, and the tiny arms which wielded the wiping-cloth with accelerated speed were bare and chapped to redness.

If it was an offence to cover a pavement with ice upon such a morning, it was a bitter wrong to compel a little child so poorly clad to perform the work.

Before Jinnie had replaced her cloth in her bucket, Mrs. Tyke appeared in the doorway with anger in her face. She took hold of one of the child's ears with her coarse fingers and pulled her into the hallway head foremost with as much force as if she had been shot out of a catapult. Then Mrs. Tyke, with a vigorous hand, boxed the ear that she had pulled, cuffed the other ear, impartially, knocking the child against the wall.

"I'll teach you to mind me when I call you! Pottering and fooling with your work! Now you go right out into the yard and scrub those bricks in a jiffy, or you'll know how the broom-handle feels."

Mrs. Tyke was going to have the back-yard scrubbed also. Why Mrs. Tyke did not scrub the four walls of the house, and the roof, and the chimney flues and the fence, and why she did not scrub the cobble-stones in the street, is an impenetrable secret.

Jinnie picked up the bucket, and went staggering through the hall, into the kitchen, with a feeling that her head might at any moment tumble off, as a result of Mrs. Tyke's blows, and roll upon the floor. She refilled her bucket at the hydrant, and began her work with a vigor that promised to make Mrs. Tyke's back-yard within a few moments a fit place for skaters.

Just before the work was done, Mrs. Tyke appeared at the window with her bonnet on, and in a severe tone gave Jinnie some directions respecting the preparation of dinner during her absence. Then Mrs. Tyke withdrew, and just as the front door slammed Jinnie saw the head of a child appear over the top of the partition fence, between the yards of Mrs. Tyke and Mrs. Brown.

Young Miss Brown watched Jinnie putting away the scrubbing implements, and when Jinnie drew near to the fence with an apparent purpose to have some conversation, the little Brown said:

"It'll pretty soon be Christmas, now."

"Will it?" said Jinnie, without manifesting any trace of interest in the fact.

"Yes, and Kris Kingle is coming to our house. Mamma said so. Does Kris Kingle come to your house on Christmas?"

"Nobody ever comes to our house but the milkman. He is not Kris Kingle, is he?"

"Oh, no! Don't you hang up your stockings on Christmas eve?"

"I have no stockings to hang up."

"Where does Kris Kingle put all your pretty things, then?"

"He don't bring me any. Who is Kris Kingle?"

"Why, don't you know? He comes in a sleigh full of toys, pulled by reindeer, and —"

"Where does he come from? Ohio?"

"I guess so. But he comes down the chimbley every night before Christmas, and —"

"I expect our chimbley must be too little. Or maybe he don't know we live here."

"Oh, he knows where everybody lives; all the little children."

"I'm *so* sorry he forgets me! Maybe it's because I have no stockings! Oh, I wish, I wish I had!"

"Won't Mrs. Tyke lend you one of hers?"

"I'm afraid to ask her. I wonder would Kris Kingle come if I put a bucket there for him?"

"I never heard of his giving toys in a bucket.

If he gave you a large doll maybe he would. Have you got a large doll?"

"I never had any doll. I made one once out of a dust brush and some rags, but Mrs. Tyke whipped me and took it away. If I had a real doll I'd be so happy that I couldn't stand it."

"If Mrs. Tyke whipped you for it that would keep you from being too happy, wouldn't it?"

"Yes."

"Why didn't you ask your mamma to write to Kris Kingle to come?"

"I never had a mamma; and no father, either. I was born in an asylum, and Mrs. Tyke always says it's a pity I was ever."

"Maybe he'd come if you'd pray to get him."

"I only know 'Now I lay me.' I learned it at the asylum; but I daren't say it out loud any more."

"I don't know what we can do about it, then."

Jinnie began to cry; but suddenly remembering the imminent probability of Mrs. Tyke's return, she wiped her eyes with a rag of her dress, and said, —

"Good-bye; I must go in now. I have to get dinner."

So she ran into the kitchen, and the head of the youthful Brown slowly descended until it was eclipsed by the fence.

Jinnie went to work to prepare the vegetables

for dinner, with her poor little brain in such a stir of excitement about Kris Kingle and the possibility of his remembering her or forgetting her, that she could hardly keep her mind upon the task that her hands were doing; but she was recalled from her dreams by the sound of Mrs. Tyke's step in the hall; and as Mrs. Tyke perceived that she had not been very industrious, Mrs. Tyke promptly boxed her ears. She fell to the floor, and then Mrs. Tyke kicked her two or three times. This energetic treatment effectively dispelled all of Jinnie's visions of Kris Kingle. She had rarely had any information upon which to build pleasant thoughts of what life might have been to her; and now when her little mind was taking its first flight into those realms of imagination wherein so many of the forlorn of earth find at least a taste of happiness, the red and vigorous hand of Mrs. Tyke hurled her back once more into the dreary and dreadful reality of life.

For the rest of the day Jinnie hurried through her myriad duties with a tremulous fear upon her that if she should dare even to think of that mysterious being who loved the little children she might invoke still further blows. The blows came at any rate, more than once, despite her carefulness; but that was always a part of her experience, and she bore them perhaps a little better now because she was looking forward with a faint suggestion of happiness to the night, when she should lie beneath the scant covering of her bed, and think without fear of harm of the reindeer and sleigh and the toys of the kind old man, who might perhaps not forget her this time.

When supper-time came Mrs. Tyke ordered her to go to the baker's for bread. The shop to which she had been accustomed to go was closed, for some reason, and Jinnie sought another, upon another street. On her way home through the dusky thoroughfare she came suddenly upon a show-window brilliantly lighted, and filled with childish splendors belonging to the Christmas season.

She had never seen so many beautiful things before. There were toys of all kinds, some of which she understood and some of which were all the more fascinating for the mystery that surrounded them. There were wagons and horses, and miniature tea-sets, and pop-guns, and baby houses, and jumping-jacks, and railroad cars, and tin steamboats, and make-believe soldier caps ; and these were mingled with clusters of glass balls of various colors, which glittered in the gaslight in a most wonderful manner. But the glory of the window was a huge waxen doll dressed as a bride, in pure white, with a veil and a wreath and the loveliest satin dress. She had real golden hair and the softest blue eyes, that stared and stared as though they were looking into some other surprising show-window over the way.

Jinnie trembled when she saw this marvellous doll. She had no idea that anybody ever wore such wonderful clothing as that. She had never dreamed that anything could be so beautiful. She thought she would be perfectly happy if she could stand there and gaze at it during the remainder of her life. Oh, if Kris Kingle would come and leave her such a doll as that! No, that could not be; it was impossible that she should ever have such a joyful experience. But maybe he might bring her a doll like some of the smaller and less splendid ones which surrounded the bride in swarms. Yes, she would be satisfied with the very poorest one of them. She would hide it somewhere, under her bed covering, perhaps, where Mrs. Tyke could not see it, but where she could find it and kiss it and hug it and take it close in her arms when she went to sleep at night.

The thought of Mrs. Tyke came to her like a blow in the midst of her delight. She remembered that she must hurry homeward, and so taking a last, long look she turned and ran along the pavement, her heart filled with a wild, passionate longing that Kris Kingle would come to her and bring her something she could love.

Of course Mrs. Tyke greeted her with angry words and two or three savage thumps. She expected that. But Mrs. Tyke was not content with this. When she sat down to supper she told Jinnie that as she had been unusually idle and bad that day she should go hungry to bed. Then Mrs. Tyke ate a particularly hearty meal, with the child watching her; and when she had finished she sat by, growling and threatening, while Jinnie cleared away the tea-things preparatory to being marched off to bed.

Jinnie missed her supper sadly, but she did not mind the hunger so much on that night, for her mind was busy with new delights.

It was dark in her room, but she knew where the chimney was; and before she undressed she went over and felt it. There was a hole there for a stove-pipe, but it had paper pasted over it.

"Perhaps," said Jinnie, "Kris Kingle did not come because the hole was shut."

He would not come down the chimney and out into the dining-room, she knew, because he would have to go through the stove; and that would burn him, and his toys, too, perhaps. She thought it might be an inducement for him to come if she should punch a hole through the paper. She was afraid to tear it off, afraid of Mrs. Tyke's vengeance; so she pushed her finger through it. Then she undressed, and went hopefully to her bed upon the floor.

But not to sleep; she was too greatly excited. She began to wonder why it was that life was so terrible. She never imagined that her life differed from those of other children. It is the peculiar infamy of brutality to a child that the victim does not know how to sound the cry for the help that is almost always near to it. It accepts its lot as a thing of course; it does not know that there are perhaps within a few short steps of its house of suffering hearts that would stir with wrath for its wrongs, and that there is within reach a law which would bring retribution upon the head of its oppressor.

Jinnie believed that all childhood was a time of punishment and misery. She saw other children playing in the street who seemed merry and joyous, and she could not understand why they were so. She remembered the Brown girl, also, and how she had heard her sometimes laughing and singing. Jinnie could not laugh and sing in her house with Mrs. Tyke near her. She thought the other children might be happy because they had dolls, and because they could have their stockings filled at Christmas time. She knew that grown-up people were not abused as she was, but it seemed such a long, long time to wait until she was grown up. She felt that when she was she would be kinder to children, and not strike them with the poker, at any rate, as Mrs. Tyke sometimes struck her.

And if Kris Kingle should come down into her room through the hole in the paper, she thought she would like to be awake and to ask him to take her away with him in his sleigh somewhere. As she dwelt upon this she pictured herself going up the chimney and then flying over the roofs behind the reindeer, and looking back at Mrs. Tyke standing at the window and cursing her. And so she fell asleep and into a tangled maze of dreams, wherein Kris Kingle, Mrs. Tyke and the doll-baby bride were mingled in great confusion.

Jinnie's first thought in the morning was the last that she had upon the night before. But as she hurriedly dressed herself it flashed across her mind that as there was grave peril that Kris Kingle might not come to her, perhaps it would make matters surer if she should go to him.

The milkman, whose cry she expected every moment, to her seemed a likely person to know where Kris lived, and to take her there. Young Miss Brown had rather indicated that Kris's home was in Ohio; but whether Ohio was a little piece up the street or millions of miles away, or whether it was a house or a stable or a town, she did not know. The milkman had spoken pleasantly to her sometimes, and he had a wagon. It was not as attractive as a sleigh with reindeer, but she had often longed to ride in it. She determined to speak to him. But when he came and she opened the door with a beating heart, he snatched the pitcher from her hand and frowned while he filled it. He was thinking of some offensive suggestions made by

Mrs. Tyke upon the preceding evening in reference to his too intense partiality for water; and he seemed so cross that Jinnie was afraid to speak to him.

She came into the house again sorrowfully, but with a strong purpose to seek some other means of reaching Kris Kingle; and she carried this determination with her stubbornly through all the fatigues and hardships of the day.

About four o'clock in the afternoon Mrs. Tyke went out. Jinnie felt that her time had come. She resolved to make an effort to find Kris Kingle, to tell him of her longing desire, and to return home again before Mrs. Tyke got back. She put her woollen hood upon her head, wrapped around her shoulders the thin and faded rag which Mrs. Tyke dignified with the name of a shawl; and then she concluded to take a newspaper with her, so that if Kris Kingle showed any disposition to urge the doll-baby upon her in advance of Christmas, she could have something to wrap it in.

When she came out of the house she crossed the street so that she could notice particularly whether there was anything in the construction of the roof of Mrs. Tyke's dwelling which would be likely to discourage Kris Kingle from attempting to reach the chimney. She saw that the roof was much lower than the roofs of the houses upon each side of it, and that it sloped at a sharp angle toward the front, while they were flat. The chimney, also, was certainly smaller than others in the vicinity, and the conclusion reached by the child's mind was that Kris Kingle had probably been indisposed to take the risks of running his sleigh upon so precipitous a roof for the sake of descending such a very narrow chimney.

This gave a fresh impulse to the child's purpose to visit Kris Kingle, so that she might plead with him to make a call at Mrs. Tyke's despite the inconveniences of the construction of the house. It occurred to her that she might possibly arrange for him to come to the front door and ring the bell, when she would come softly down stairs and open to receive him.

While she thought of the matter she walked quickly up the street, now somewhat gloomy in the early dusk, but before she had gone far she reflected that she ought to inquire the way to Ohio before the darkness should come. She paused to speak to two or three men who were hurrying by, but evidently they thought she intended to ask alms of them, and so they would not pause to listen to her. She was discouraged; but at last she saw a boy standing by a street lamp, doing nothing, and she resolved to ask him.

He laughed rudely at her question and walked away. A moment later he turned and threw a snowball at her. It hit her in the face and hurt her badly; and her foot slipping upon the icy pavement, she fell. A moment elapsed before she was able to rise; but at last she got up, and although she was cold and weak and greatly discouraged, she thought she would press on. She might never have so good a chance again; and if she did not see Kris Kingle now, Christmas would come, and he would come and go, and there would be no doll for her.

While she was standing there, in a very miserable frame of mind, a nicely dressed lady went past her. Presently the lady turned and looked at her; then she came back to where Jinnie stood and spoke to her.

"What is your name, my child?" asked the lady.

"Virginia, ma'am. But Mrs. Tyke generally calls me Jinnie." She had never heard so sweet a voice. It seemed so beautiful, so gentle, so full of tender pity, that it thrilled her with a strange joy.

"And where are you going?"

"I am going out to Ohio, to see Kris Kingle."

The lady smiled; but the smile faded into a look of deep compassion, and she said, —

"Did your mother let you come away from home?"

"I have no mother. I'm a bound girl."

"Who sent you to find Kris Kingle?"

"Nobody. He always forgets to come to our house, so I was goin' to put him in mind."

"Don't you get any toys or candy on Christmas?"

"No, ma'am. Mrs. Tyke won't give me any, and Kris Kingle forgets me. And I never tasted candy but once."

"Is Mrs. Tyke the woman you live with?"

"Yes, ma'am."

"Does she treat you kindly?"

"Whips me and knocks me down sometimes."

"Will you go back to her?"

"Oh yes, ma'am. I am going right back as soon as I see Kris Kingle."

The lady took her hand and resolved to go back with her, and to see the terrible Mrs. Tyke. She told Jinnie so, and Jinnie submitted, although she was grieved to forego her errand.

"Do you know who Kris Kingle really is?" the lady asked.

"Yes; he brings nice things down the chimbley to children."

"He does better things than that, my dear. The real Kris Kingle is the Christ-child."

"Who is He?"

"Did you never hear anybody tell of Christ?"

"No, ma'am."

"He is God. He came down here to live upon earth, where He suffered and died for us. He loved little children, for He was Himself once a child."

"Was He little, like me?"

"Yes."

"How did He suffer?"

"Wicked men insulted Him and beat Him and killed Him."

"Did they beat Him and strike Him like they do me?"

"Yes, my poor child."

"What makes Him love me? Because I am beaten just like He was?"

"Yes, yes, that is it. But He loves everybody, good and bad."

"He doesn't know Mrs. Tyke, does He?"

"He knows everybody in the world."

"Where is He now?"

"Up in Heaven?"

"Is that farther than Ohio?"

"Yes, that is far, far away in the skies."

"Then how does He get here? I always thought the real Kris Kingle came down chimbleys."

"He comes in your heart, my dear child. You will understand it all some day."

The lady seemed strangely moved as she said this to Jinnie; but she said nothing, and led Jinnie through the street, towards the child's home.

When Jinnie and her companion reached Mrs. Tyke's house and rang the bell, Mrs. Tyke herself came to the door and opened it. As soon as she saw Jinnie she poured out at her a volley of abusive words, without regarding the presence of the lady who accompanied her. The lady remonstrated with Mrs. Tyke, and then Mrs. Tyke assailed her with her tongue. The lady then told Mrs. Tyke that she knew of the cruel treatment to which the child had been subjected, and that she would interfere if it was repeated.

Jinnie was astonished that any one should be so bold as to speak with so much severity to Mrs. Tyke. The response made to this threat by Mrs. Tyke was to seize Jinnie by the arm, to drag her suddenly into the hallway, and to slam the door in the lady's face.

The lady stood upon the step and listened. She could hear Mrs. Tyke beating the child and cursing her; and then the sounds receded, as if Mrs. Tyke were dragging Jinnie into a room at the end of the hallway. Mrs. Tyke was in a paroxysm of fury; and she intended to visit upon Jinnie the vengeance she would have liked to inflict upon Jinnie's unknown friend.

Beating was too common and too tame a form of punishment. Mrs. Tyke's ingenuity devised a more terrible one. She made the child remove her shoes, and then she tied her upon a chair, with her naked feet within a few inches of the hot stove. In that position she left Jinnie, who bore the frightful pain bravely, until presently she fainted.

If there is no hell, what is going to become of people like Mrs. Tyke?

When Jinnie regained consciousness, Mrs. Tyke sternly ordered her to go up to bed; and Jinnie crawled up the staircase slowly and painfully upon her hands and knees, suffering so much that she could hardly help screaming aloud.

She reached her room at last, and flung herself down upon the bed. Her pain was so great that it was a long while before she could go to sleep; and she lay there thinking with all her might about Kris Kingle and the doll baby, and her adventures in the street, and wondering if she would ever be any happier. Then she remembered what little Miss Brown had said about praying, and what the sweet lady had told her about the Christ-child and His wondrous love; and so she thought she would try to pray to Him; and praying, she fell asleep.

The lady who brought Jinnie home turned away with her soul filled with indignation at Mrs. Tyke's cruelty to the child, and she determined to have it ended. She knew a man, Thomas Elwood, who was active in the service of the Society for Protecting Children from Cruelty, and she went to his house. He was a very plain Friend; a young man, and of a fair countenance. He was at home with his wife, and both expressed deep interest in the visitor's story. The visitor left with the assurance from Elwood that the case would receive attention early the next morning.

Next morning, when Mrs. Tyke called Jinnie, Jinnie tried to rise, but found that she could not: she was too feeble and wretched. Mrs. Tyke saw this, and she did not compel Jinnie to get up. Mrs. Tyke was beginning to be frightened. So Jinnie fell asleep again, and when she awoke it was broad daylight, and a man with what seemed to be an angelic face was standing beside her. It was Thomas Elwood. Jinnie was startled; her first impression was that this was Kris Kingle, come in answer to her prayer. But when Jinnie looked at the finger-hole she had made in the fire-board and at the man, and particularly at the circumference of his hat, it seemed to her impossible, if this was Kris Kingle, that he should have come in by way of Mrs. Tyke's chimney.

Thomas Elwood spoke to her and asked her if she suffered much. She said yes, and then she asked him if he really was Kris Kingle.

Thomas smiled and said, —

"No, dear child; but I am thy friend, and I am going to take thee away from this misery and keep thee until thee is well again."

Then he lifted Jinnie in his arms, bore her downstairs and out, and placed her in a carriage.

"Where is Mrs. Tyke?" thought Jinnie. Mrs. Tyke was at a magistrate's office, listening to Mrs.

Brown and others of the neighbors while they testified of her brutal treatment of Jinnie. The lady who had brought Jinnie home was there also; and Jinnie was kindly pressed by the magistrate to tell what Mrs. Tyke had done to her.

Mrs. Tyke gave bail and went home. Thomas Elwood took Jinnie to his own house, and his wife wept as he told her how the child had been tortured. She carried Jinnie upstairs and washed her, and dressed her in clothes that Jinnie thought were wonderful, though they were so plain. Then she kissed Jinnie and said to her, —

"I once had a little girl of thy age; but a year ago she died. She even looked like thee, my dear."

Jinnie was so weak that she had to lie upon the bed when the washing and dressing were over; "and such a bed!" thought Jinnie. Thomas Elwood's wife brought some breakfast up to her, and Jinnie thought that she had never tasted anything so good. She did not know that such delicious food could be found anywhere in the world.

Jinnie grew better and stronger in a few days, and Thomas Elwood and his wife became so much attached to her that they resolved that they would keep her and adopt her in the place of the child that had been taken away from them.

Jinnie was very happy, and she talked freely with them. She told them about her search for Kris Kingle, and about that splendid doll she saw in the window on the night she went to the strange baker's.

Although entertaining sentiments which forbade any enthusiasm for Christmas and Kris Kingle, and dolls in gorgeous apparel, something impelled Thomas Elwood to go to see that special doll.

That night, as he sat with his wife in front of the grate fire in the sitting-room, she said to him, Jinnie being in bed, —

"Thomas, does thee think there would be any harm in giving Virginia a little pleasure on the 25th of this month?"

"How does thee mean, Rachel?"

"Well, she seems to have her little head filled with nonsense about Kris Kingle and Christmas, and as the poor child has had a life so full of misery, I thought, perhaps, we might —"

"Thee does n't mean to keep Christmas in this house, does thee?"

"Not exactly that, but —"

"What would Friends say if we should do that?"

"No; but there can be no harm in giving the poor child some playthings, and we may as well give them upon one day as another."

"What kind of playthings would thee give her?"

"Why not buy her a doll? She seemed to like that doll at Thomas Smith's store very much."

"But, Rachel, that doll was dressed in a most worldly manner. Ought we to risk filling the child's mind with vain and frivolous notions about dress?"

"She has hardly had a chance to feed her vanity in that manner thus far."

"Thee would be willing, then," said Thomas, "to buy for her that gaily-dressed doll?"

"I think I would; just this once."

"Well," said Thomas, slowly, "I am glad to hear thee say so, because to-day I bought that very doll." And he produced it from a bundle that he took from under the sofa.

Kris Kingle came to Jinnie that Christmas eve, and in the morning her joy as she clasped the doll in her arms was so great that she could not express it. While she was at the breakfast table Thomas Elwood was called to the parlor to see a visitor. Presently he summoned Jinnie, and when Jinnie came into the room she was startled to see Mrs. Tyke. It flashed across her mind that Mrs. Tyke had come to take her away, and she began to cry. Thomas Elwood comforted her. Mrs. Tyke had come to beg for mercy. She wished to escape prosecution.

Thomas turned to Jinnie and said, —

"Virginia, this is the woman who has done thee so much harm. I can have her punished if I wish. What would thee do to her if thee had thy way?"

"I would forgive her," said Jinnie, timidly.

It seemed as if Jinnie had been visited also by the *real* Kris Kingle. Mrs. Tyke was permitted to go unpunished.

www.ingramcontent.com/pod-product-compliance
Lightning Source LLC
Chambersburg PA
CBHW030320240426
43673CB00040B/1229